HOW TO TELL IF SOMEONE IS LYING

GAVIN STONE REVEALS THE METHODS USED BY GOVERNMENT ORGANIZATIONS & INTELLIGENCE AGENCIES TO DETECT LIES!

(SECOND EDITION)

BY

GAVIN STONE

A half-truth is still a whole lie.

With special thanks to:

Philip Ingram MBE – Former senior intelligence officer for British Military Intelligence & founder of Grey Hare Media

Lena Sisco – Former U.S. Naval Intelligence, Author, Military Interrogation & lie detection expert.

Matthew Dunn – Former MI6 Intelligence Officer & Author

Thomas Pecora – Former CIA Intelligence officer & Author

Eric Hunley – Former U.S. Army & host of the popular shows;

Eric Hunley Unstructured & Americas Untold Stories.

James (Jim) Pyle – Former U.S. Army Interrogator & Law Enforcement Training Instructor

Anonymous 1 - Intelligence officer MI5 (Still active)

Anonymous 2 – Intelligence Analyst GCHQ (Still active)

Anonymous 3 – Former British special forces SBS (Retired)

All of my friends and associates in the Military, Security & Intelligence Community,

My fellow authors who have shown great support,

And lastly but by no means least,

My wife and daughter who complete my world.

Original Cover design (First edition) by: oliviaprodesign

<u>Beta reading:</u>

<u>(First edition)</u>

Phill Lovelock
Ben Wynne
& Chelsey Golledge

<u>(Second edition)</u>

Chloe McDonald
Bryon Jaffee

<u>Editing by:</u>

Julia Krzyzanowska

<u>Proof reading by:</u>

Angie Graham &
Julia Krzyzanowska

<u>**Second Edition**</u>

Second Edition Audiobook Narrated by: Eric Hunley

Contents

Foreword By Matthew Dunn

When I joined Great Britain's Secret Intelligence Service, commonly known as MI6, the subsequent training program was exacting, multifaceted, and ingenious. And yet only part of the program was "training". New recruits were taught world-leading espionage tradecraft, techniques, including anti-surveillance, covert infiltration and exfiltration, small arms, aggressive driving, explosives, unarmed combat, and all the other flash-bang spy-stuff that is hugely exciting but must be ingrained in order to avoid imprisonment or death. The rest of the program was different and was designed to enable recruits to become who they were born to be – spies. Within that dynamic, the minds of MI6 recruits weren't tinkered with. They were encouraged, for sure, but the view of senior MI6 instructors was that they'd invested in the diverse high-speed brains of their recruits and, as a result, they didn't want to tell them how to think. We weren't advised to read books on lying and other topics which attempt to decipher the machinations of the human mind. Such books would have, at best, been written- off as stifling intuitive and creative thought and, at worst, been deemed utter tosh. MI6 relies on the brilliance of its recruits and pays no attention to the latest theories of psychologists, behavior gurus, and other so-called "experts". It paves its own way through the human condition and is more likely to recruit someone who studied a degree in Byzantine Literature than an individual who spent years pouring over books on social and cognitive science.

But, on very rare occasions a body of work comes along that should prompt the likes of MI6 to take note. Stone's "How To Tell If

Someone is Lying" is such a book. It is real, accurate and written by someone who is superbly placed to impart his knowledge to people from all walks of life. In his gritty career, Stone has rolled up his sleeves to get his job done amid the most exotic climes to the dingiest back alleys and numerous places in-between. He's never cared which people he has to mix with, so long as he succeeds with his task. As a result, he

knows people. That knowledge is so wide-ranging that it makes his book incredibly relatable.

This isn't just a book that my old pals in MI6 should read. It's a book for everyone who wants to go about their daily lives while trying to work out if people who matter to them are telling them fibs.

The relatable and expert aspects of Stone's book are not its only unusual components. There's a third pillar to this work of non-fiction, and that pillar's a mighty one – application. Most of us are busy people who want solutions to problems we encounter. At every stage in this book, Stone applies solutions, and he does so in an honest and no-nonsense way. He's a realist. He gets that people are different. And yet he's able to show us brilliantly simple techniques that can be directed towards anyone, regardless as to whether they're a deceitful business partner, cheating spouse, backstabbing friend, criminal, unscrupulous salesperson, election candidate, mischievous child or government traitor. Stone identifies the minefield. And then he tells us how to navigate our way through that field. He's our guide.

And he's a charming and down-to-earth guide at that. I hope you enjoy his company as much as I did.

Matthew Dunn, June 2022

1. Introduction

If someone is lying, they do something to tell you, everyone does. The problem is it's not the same thing for every person. That's why so many people find it hard to spot when someone is lying to them. Sometimes they have this niggling feeling and they know a person is being insincere but not why. Well, this book will not only show you how to succeed in identifying the "tells" so you can fit them to each person and spot deception as plain as day; it will also teach you the proven methods used to profile people, teach you how to read body language, how to analyze a person's statements. It will show you how to avoid misreading a situation. It will explain why people will always end up talking and how to use it to your advantage. You'll know how to get someone to tell you the whole truth, as well as what questions to ask before, during and right after a confession to make sure you get all of the information. It's all crammed in here along with a lot more to help you master spotting deception and have all the tools you need at your disposal.

You will have the knowledge and will have learned HOW TO TELL IF SOMEONE IS LYING.

We will also do a bit of myth-busting and as an extra bonus you'll get to learn how to beat a polygraph lie detector!

So, who am I and how do I know all of this stuff?

My name is Gavin Stone. I'm a former Civil Servant for the British Ministry of Defense and Ex Security and Intelligence contractor, turned trainer, teacher, and instructor. I have run online courses, in addition to having trained recruits and experienced operatives for the government and private sector, and I am also currently working on building my career as an author. If you'd like to show support and be kept up to date with other upcoming events, courses, and books, please follow me on the major social media sites and also check out my website.

gavinstoneauthor.com

gavinstone.us

Facebook: Gavin Stone Author

Twitter: @AuthorGavin

Instagram: gavin_stone1

And of course, it means a lot to any author to get a review. It helps with discovery and can also assist potential customers to make a purchase. So, if you do leave a review, please know that I am extremely grateful.

Thank you in advance for your support.

Now to go a little deeper into my history. This is purely to help you understand how I managed to gain skills from a spectrum of areas and piece them together to gain the knowledge I have in my toolbox of techniques. For anyone who's ever read the epic Greek poem The Odyssey, they will know that Odysseus is not the skilled fighter like Achilles. He doesn't have the archery skills of Apollo or the speed of Hermes. The truth is, he's not the best at anything. However, his overall skillset in all these areas makes him unrivalled. It's his array of skills that makes him who he is. In the same sense my varied background in a number of professions (none the same but all related) has given me the same advantage. I consider myself a bit of a "Jack of all trades, master of none". The Odyssey is 12,109 lines long and begins in the middle of the overall story, with prior events described through flashbacks and storytelling. The 24 books correspond to the letters of the Greek alphabet; it's believed that the division was likely made after the poem's composition by someone other than Homer, but it is generally accepted that way. It's the numerous trials and multiple areas Odysseus had to adapt to that are most relevant. It's the combination of his skills that makes him so exceptional, not any single one of them in isolation. Not only does that relate to my career, but it relates to the content of this book too. I'll explain the reason for this now. Every section in this book is vital, and each of the skills on their own are worthy of credit. The combination of all of them put together, however, has the potential to make you outstanding in the area of deception detection. I'll explain further how I managed to get experience in so many areas of my working life and how it's relevant to this book.

I started right at the very bottom of the industry packet, when a friend knocked on my door one day. He told me I was the most resourceful person he knew, and he needed my help with something. The thought of a challenge intrigued me, and I was in. He went on to tell me he needed to find a person and had less than a week to do it. He gave me the information he had, and I went to work. I'm proud to say that not only did I do it, but it didn't take me a week, or a day. In fact, it took me less than an hour. Job done start to finish.

I didn't give it too much thought after that until the beginning of the next month when there was another knock at the door, and my friend handed me an envelope full of cash! I asked what it was for, and he told me it was my cut for finding the person he wanted to locate. To say I was impressed at this easy money was an understatement, and I wanted to know more. It turns out I was doing something called process serving (sometimes called a per-serve). For those who don't know what it is, it's simply finding a person and handing them documents in a sealed envelope. You personally serve them the documentation, hence the name per-serve. You are usually hired by lawyers who want to issue a court summons. There can be other reasons but most of the time, that's the main reason.

It generally happens when a summons has been sent through the post and the recipient decides to write "not at this address" on the envelope in a futile attempt to foil the sender. The number one rule I learned in this game was that the target was usually at the address from where the package was returned. Most of the time you don't have to look past the last address on record to find your target.

As you can imagine, I soon worked my way into the trade and was pretty good at it. As time went by, the bread-and-butter jobs went from people-tracing to missing persons. Marital investigations and fraud cases, as well as many other private investigation cases. In the UK you don't need a license to be a private investigator, you can simply buy a good camera, have some business cards printed, and away you go. I branched out into other areas, such as security, and learned the art of close protection and the many related areas to that too. Close protection in itself has many branches. From red carpet work to hostile environment. Celebrity work and high net worth clients, to witness protection and victims of domestic abuse, where you have an obligation to provide a safe house and protection until a pending court case. There are other areas as well, such as Maritime close protection, working on expensive vessels and providing protection from pirates and even residential security too. My job undertaking short term contracts and providing temporary cover for things like vacation leave etc. allowed me to work in many of these areas and learn from each of them, while still taking on investigative cases between contracts. The main reason I managed to work in so many areas and positions in my working life was down to the fact that I mostly offered temporary cover (Sometime called TDY – Temporary Duty). Some contracts were weeks or months long and some as short as covering for someone for as little as one day. I still give credit to my broker now for managing to find me an almost constant supply of roles to fill, with very little in the way of gaps between them. The time between contracts I managed to fill by helping out at my father's business, where most of his regular customers thought I just had many vacations. The rest of the time I continued with investigations, as and when the phone rang with the next job.

Before long I was looking into insurance fraud claims which soon progressed to benefit fraud claims for the government. I worked my way into the lives of the right people in order to achieve better contracts and take on new areas and, ultimately, new challenges. I took on jobs doing physical penetration testing, on everything from military camps to the homes and businesses of some very influential clients. My time working in security allowed me to spot the areas of weakness and flaws in other people's security. I had learned the vulnerable spots that thieves look for to break into places, so I had also learned to identify them, giving me the foundation for penetration testing skills. I soon perfected the art of CMOE (Covert Method of Entry) and was a master of surreptitious entry (becoming a qualified locksmith in the process). I'm proud to say this is an area in which I have never failed. I have always managed to gain access to, or enter any building, house, or compound, that I have been tasked to. This skill helped me in other areas, which we will cover later.

From there I went on to work freelance for training companies as well. Training personnel appointed by the government, in a mixture of areas when called upon, to assist new recruits preparing to work in the field. This in many ways helped me form the concept for this book. Teaching skills to people is a wonderful opportunity, but it is limited to one class at a time; putting the methods into a book makes them available to anyone, anywhere around the world at any time.

As I became more established in the industry, I took on more contracts for the government, more contracts from my broker, and more contracts from the Ministry of Defense. The entire time I was always envious of the full-time staff, who benefitted from things I didn't, such as paid time off, a pension, and other perks. I was only a civilian contractor, so it was simple; if I didn't work, I didn't eat. The money was good, but if I stopped for a break, so did the pay. After many years I managed to find the right person in my life to get me on the books full-time as a civil servant for the MoD (The UK version of the DOD in the US). I was over the moon. The whole process seemed to take ages, it was around 12 months of background checks and so on, before I finally signed the OSA (Official Secrets Act) once again, got my security clearance, and was able to get to work. I did it. I achieved what I'd always wanted. I had finally got what I had been so envious of for so many years. And after a few short months, I can't tell you how much I hated it!

Yep, that's right. The greener grass was not all I expected it to be. I stuck it out for a short while, but it wasn't long before I had to go back to what I did best. Working on my own, taking on short-term contracts, and exploring other options that offered fresh challenges.

This wake-up call made me stop and think. I wasn't getting any younger, the kind of work I'd done previously was far better suited to someone with youth on their side and definitely not for a family man. I'd also been very lucky; if you keep putting your hand into the fire, sooner or later, you get burned. So, I decided to make the decision to play a less active role in the Security & Intelligence industry, and on top of that, I wanted to teach my daughter as much as I could too. It was at this point that I decided to push my writing career harder and investigate the possibility of creating online courses as well. I got in touch with a friend from MI6, the British Secret Intelligence Service, and put a proposal forward to partner up and build a course offering to teach spy skills to the civilian world. I then sat down and started to type out some of what I'd learned. In effect, the creation of this book was twofold; to pass lessons on both to my daughter and the general public around the world who would also get the benefit of it.

In short, less than one percent of the people in the world have the qualifications training and experience, that allows them to come close to doing what I can! It's a bold statement but it's true and now you get to benefit from what I have learned too!

Now you know a little more about my background and you'll see how each of these areas (and some others) come into play in connection with the lessons within this book.

2. The Importance of Congruency

There's a very good reason for starting the book with this subject. I cannot over-emphasize the importance of finding a person's baseline, otherwise known as what is normal for them. If you do not know a person's baseline, then you will never know if they deviate from it. Moreover, it forms the foundation for every section of this book, from body language to the analysis of a person's statement, and everything in between. When you're trying to detect lies, what you really need to look for is change. In order to spot change, you need to be able to identify what exactly is different, in order to find out why.

When a CIA operative gets trained at the Farm (Camp Peary, Langley Virginia) there's a particular phrase that's said over and over. Its use is repetitive, so many times a day that it has almost become the camp's unofficial mantra.

That phrase is simply, "it depends."

The reason I bring this up is because I get asked many times, "a person has made X particular action, what does it mean?"

And the answer is simple. As they say on the Farm, it depends. It depends on if that action is normal for that person. It depends on the circumstances that person is in. It depends on a whole bunch of things. Before you can explore any of them though, more importantly than anything, you must know the person's baseline.

With my knowledge of body language, I regularly get asked questions like, "if a person crosses their legs when they sit down, what does it mean?" And I usually answer, "It means they crossed their legs".

What so many people fail to understand is that there is no "Body Language Dictionary" that offers a literal "this action equals that thought" translation. There are so many actions a person can take that will mean one thing for one person and something completely different for someone else. It's almost like learning a new language every time you speak to a new person. I will explain how to simplify it though, and by the end of this book you'll have the tools to create a mental record of a person's baseline effectively and efficiently. It's easily done, and we will revisit this in other sections of the book where it applies to each individual skill.

With all said and done, there are some particular traits and actions that are as close to universal as you can get when it comes to some areas of body language. We will cover these later, but for now, I want to stress yet again the importance of finding a person's baseline and also to state that this book is not a body language book; it's a book to teach you the skill of being able to tell when someone is lying. Body language, though, does play a vital role. It's no more or less important than any other skill. As previously mentioned, it's the combination of all the components together that will give you the overall skillset.

While I'm covering the basics, I feel it's important also to point out that there's a huge difference between knowledge and skill. Knowing is one thing, but applying it is something completely different. I have said before that having the ingredients does not give you the recipe. I don't know about you, but I'd rather have a pilot that's flown a plane a hundred times successfully and never read a book about it than a pilot who's read a hundred books on how to fly but has never actually flown a plane. I hope that makes sense, and that I have explained the difference between knowledge and skill in a way that puts it into perspective. Now that I've highlighted this little fact, I want you to keep it in mind when we later go on to cover the application of what you've learned. I don't feel it's addressed enough. So many people read books or watch YouTube videos through which they have gained knowledge, but these books and videos let you down. They give you the information but don't teach you how to go out and apply it in the real world. As you read through this book you will gain an understanding of some techniques that will have you going out into the world and applying what you've learned from the ground up, so that you can build up to expert level and have a sound footing from the start.

There's a U.S. Military acronym BOB which stands for Brilliant on Basics, and this is where we need to start off. You have to look at this whole thing like learning a new language, because effectively, it is. Therefore, it goes without saying that you can't expect to read a book and be fluent. The secret is to get BOB. What I would suggest is to start with one particular item on our checklist that you will actively go out and look for every time you interact with others, whether it's in person, online, or even on the television. Have you ever noticed that when you buy a new car, you seem to see them everywhere? It's

13

not because suddenly everyone else went out and bought the same car. It's because your brain has figured out that it's important to you. A mixture of emotions and thoughts have literally sent a signal to your subconscious to say this purchase was an important part of your life and the car itself is highly relevant. The result? Your subconscious makes a note of how important this car is and sends a signal to your conscious mind every time you spot one, highlighting its presence. Whereas you probably wouldn't have even noticed it before, now you get that little silent alarm going off in your head every time one drives past you. When you condition your brain to look for something, the same effect is achieved. Your subconscious mind eventually gets the message of its importance and sooner or later, you start spotting it automatically. You won't even need to do the work, it will just happen.

When you have reached this level of unconscious competence with one item on the checklist (it will happen sooner that you think), you can work on the next item on the checklist. It may sound slow and tedious, but I can assure you that the process will not only speed up each and every time you do it; it will also click into place and stick a lot better than if you try to read the entire book and go out into the world expecting to be fluent in what you've learned. Imagine someone who doesn't know Spanish reading a Spanish phrase book from start to finish and then getting frustrated because when they go out, they can't remember the entire language and fluently order Tequila and Burritos at a Mexican restaurant! It's insane, isn't it? So why would body language (or any of the other skills in this book) be any different?

So, take it from me, start by learning how to say "Hola". Learn the basics. Practice each item on the checklist one at a time until you've mastered it, then move to the next. If you want to speed the process up even more, then use a little traditional conditioning technique. Set yourself a goal to spot a particular action or trait on the list, and every time you interact with people and spot it, give yourself a treat. I'm not necessarily saying you should walk around with a bag of Scooby Snacks. It doesn't need to be chocolates or candy (although it could be if you like), a simple pat on the back or just congratulating yourself will do. If you don't feel it's enough and don't fancy the idea of risking diabetes, then try a points system. Give yourself a point every time you spot what you're looking for and make yourself a promise that when you get to a certain number of points, you'll treat yourself to gift. Maybe something off your wish list. I will add that if you decide to make it a high number of points for a slightly bigger gift, or if your memory for this kind of thing isn't as good as it should be, then maybe keep a scorecard and a pencil in your pocket so you don't lose track. You may come up with a different system that works better for you, but remember, you're better off learning in small chunks working on one item at a time. Too much at once can be overwhelming and cause you to give it up. For a higher level of success, learning a little at a time slowly is better than learning nothing because you bit off more than you could chew. As I frequently say to my daughter, slow progress is better than no progress.

I hope this has inspired you to take it step-by-step and get it right. We live in an age of information overload. Never in history has all the working knowledge in the world been so easily accessible for so many. This in itself can create information overload and the desire to take in as much as you can as quickly as possible. It's going to be down to you to regulate what you read and learn to apply it before moving on to the next step at a controlled pace.

Writing a page turner is the dream of most authors who want to write a book that the reader can't put down, and of course I want you to enjoy this book. But I also want you to absorb what it has to teach, and most importantly, I want you to learn from it. That's why throughout the book I'll come up with scenarios, examples, or short stories in each section, to try and assist you as best I can to remember the lessons from each section.

The current understanding is that there are two ways memories are created. Nearly every memory you have is tied to an emotion (the same part of the brain that stores emotions is also where memories are stored). One way or another, there is an emotional connection with everything you remember that is stored in your long-term memory. Therefore, if you want to remember something, you need to create a strong emotional link to the memory you're trying to retain. Thus, as you go through this book, each time you learn something new, think about how it relates to you and your life. Create a strong emotional story that you can tell yourself, or think of a way in which the skill could possibly have helped you in the past at a pivotal point in your life. Imagine how differently your life could have turned out if you had the ability to spot when a particular person had lied to you, and the impact that would have had on you and your circumstances now.

The second way memories enter our long-term storage system is through novelty. If our brain is entertained as we learn, the information seems to stay put a lot quicker and lot more effectively than if we just use the old-fashioned repetition technique. While I'll do my best to keep this book as entertaining as I can, it is written primarily as a self-help style educational book to teach you how to spot a liar. With that in mind, as you complete each section, if you can't think of a way you could have used each lesson in the past in a way that has a strong emotional link, try to think of a way you might be able to use it in the future that ties it into a scenario with a novelty factor. Create a situation in your head that's funny, entertaining, intriguing, and most importantly silly! Very, very silly. As extreme and as out there as you can make it. I know it sounds childish but here's the thing, who are the fastest learners in the world? Children.

Therefore, when you dream up a scenario that you tie to each skill, make it as extreme and as out there as possible. Let your imagination run wild and come up with the most vivid situations possible that would allow you to see yourself using the skill and how it would impact you and the world around you. It really will help you to remember it, especially if you over-exaggerate the particular action you're looking for to extremes. For example, something as little as a lady running her finger through her hair to slide it behind her ear could be an opportunity to use your imagination to picture her ear growing huge on the side of her face and then tie it to what it could possibly mean by picturing the meaning in a similar and equally extreme way. So, do you know what it means when a girl slips her hair behind her ear? Well, if you were paying attention earlier, you should have answered, "it depends!"

Hopefully these two little insights will not only help you take advantage of the content of this book, but it will also assist in other areas of your life where you want to learn or remember important information.

Before we move on, I'm going to give you another way to sharpen your skills. As I mentioned earlier, the importance of baselining is critical. You do that by noting what is normal for a particular person, and that is achieved by the recognition of patterns. By noting how the person reacts in each situation you can tell if that's how they normally react or if they have deviated from their standard reaction. A great way to get exceptionally skilled at this is to make predictions.

When you sit back and observe, you can learn so much. So at every opportunity, simply watch and predict the outcome, then as it unfolds, see if your prediction is correct. Let's imagine a situation where a guy in the office you work in tells you he's going to ask the new girl on a date. Stay far enough away to observe without hearing a word they say. Watch the body language and see if you can pinpoint the moment at which he gets either a yes or a no. I bet you will surprise yourself at how good you are; you'll find you know exactly what the answer is before he comes back and tells you. Of course, there are plenty of scenarios where you can use the same technique to sharpen and improve these skills, getting better with each try.

Eventually, you could to go practically anywhere and read the room. You'll be able to look at groups of people and know by how they're standing if they've recently met or are old friends. You'll be able to tell which ones want more and which ones are keen to get away, which ones are engaged, and so on. By predicting their next action, you will be able to confirm your thoughts. If you watch a group and the ones you predicted excuse themselves at the first opportunity, then you can give yourself a pat on the back. Once again, I reckon you'll surprise yourself at how good at this you are, and it will give you the confidence to continue. Assess the reasons for your beliefs and why you told yourself "I knew it!" after the event. What was it that caused you to make that specific prediction? Each time watch a little closer until you find yourself homing in on all the tiny details and pinpointing the exact actions made that drew you to create your prediction.

With enough practice and the right recurring results, combined with your assessment of each situation being analyzed to the point where you can accurately state exactly what made you make the prediction you did; you will find you can reach expert level for reading people in a very short time. We as humans are naturally good at this kind of thing anyway. Most of the time we can make predictions, and many times people say the words, "I knew it". The only issue is, they might have known it but didn't know *how* they knew it. This is why you have to reverse-engineer the process and figure out the reasons behind your prediction, comparing the results each time.

I hope all this makes sense to you, and with the techniques I mentioned you can go out into as many situations as you can throw yourself into and do a bit of people-watching, becoming better at reading them each time.

Before we move on, another worthwhile action is to journal your observations. Writing them will help reinforce the link to the memory, and it has been proven that people who journal, process thoughts faster. In fact, journaling in general can be considered a form of outlet for things like stress too. Suppression can result in health problems such as heart problems, so not only will it help you to learn but it could benefit your health too. Just another of the many little tips and bonuses that will be peppered throughout this book for you. I hope you find value in them.

3. Methods of Revealing Guilt

This is going to be a lot easier than you expect. It's one of the first methods I've put in here because you can learn it, remember it, and use it with very little exertion. It's that simple. You don't need huge amounts of practice; you can literally read it now and apply it straight away. You can practice a few times and then simply drop it into your arsenal of weapons for deception detection, ready to pull out and use as and when you need it.

You're probably thinking it sounds easy, well, that's because it is. Not only is it easy but it works on pretty much everybody. Irrelevant to the person's age or the circumstances, you can use this method to reveal whether a person's guilty or not, and it works every single time. Or at least, it has for me so far.

It works like this: imagine you're a cop, and you're interviewing a suspected rapist. You're pretty certain he did it but want to confirm your thoughts. You simply ask this question:

"What do you think should happen to the person that did this?"

That one simple line is all it takes. Now all you do is listen to their response. If they start to tell you that the guilty party should be strung up or put to death or given some seriously harsh punishment, then there is a high chance it wasn't them. If you really believe that they did it, however, then there's something completely different you should be listening for.

What you're listening for is lenience. If they start telling you that maybe the guy should get counselling or they start to suggest that there may have been extenuating circumstances or anything that could be considered a means of lessening the severity of punishment the guilty person deserves, then I'd bet almost anything that they did it.

Like I said, you can use this on anyone of any age. Imagine a scenario where two siblings break a vase in the living room when playing ball. They could be twins or of similar age, it doesn't really matter, but you separate them and ask each of them in turn, what they think should be done to the person who broke the vase. The first child responds with:

"I don't know. No more ball in the house, I guess."

But the second child responds like this:

"No allowance for a month, more chores, no video games for a week, no privileges, they have to give up their cell phone, they have to stay in all weekend."

And so on. You can bet safely that it was the first child who broke the vase.

When I first learned about this method, I thought *surely it can't be that simple?* But it is. Probably like you are doing now, I was thinking that anyone with a reasonable level of intellect would realize they're being manipulated into an all-revealing response. With that in mind, when I tried it for the first time, I was shocked at how simple and effective it was. The person I tested it on was a highly educated individual, and I expected him to look at me and tell me I wasn't going to catch him out that easily. So when he gave the revealing response that he did, I was amazed. It worked, and it worked well. I've tested it on many occasions, in several ways, and on multiple types of people through a spectrum of ages, sexes, and intelligence levels etc., and it worked every time.

I think the first time I learned about it was through the eminent Chase Hughes, so all the credit for this technique goes to him. If you haven't already read his books, then I highly recommend them. He has non-fiction books on profiling that are the best I have ever come across, *Six Minute X-Ray* being a case in point, and fiction novels where he can get away with revealing a little more through the story if you read between the lines. So, if this kind of thing interests you, then Chase's books are some I'd recommend for you next.

The next method of revealing guilt (which can also lead to a confession if executed correctly) is creating the element of doubt in the person being questioned.

Once again, I'm going to create a scenario for you to see the possible ways a line of questioning might achieve certain results and why. There are several methods we could use alongside the one I'm trying to highlight here, but for the sake of not over-complicating things, I'm just going to concentrate on the one for the moment. When you've taken this one in, we can look at adding the others. Remember, it's the combination of all the lessons together that will bring you up to expert level.

Let's say Maddison is married to Randy and believes Randy is cheating with the office junior, Chloe, from his work. She suspects they stayed in a hotel last night, and Randy lied about being out with the guys for a few drinks. Let's assume the hotel is over the north side of town, and the bar that Randy said he was drinking in is over the south side of town.

Maddison begins to question her husband, and the conversation goes a little something like this:

M) "Did you stay in a hotel with Chloe last night?"

R) "Don't be absurd! I told you I was out drinking with the boys."

If Maddison persists down this line of questioning, she will simply become stuck in the 'quicksand effect' which we will cover later. Instead, her questioning should go something more like this:

M) "So how was your night out with the lads?" (Keeping the tone light and inquisitive)

R) "Yeah, it was a good night, I had a lot of fun"

M) "Over the south side of town, right?" (Remaining in the same light tone constantly)

R) "Yeah, that's right."

M) "So, is there any reason your car might have been seen on the north side of town, honey?"

At this moment, Maddison has not revealed that his car *was* seen there *or* by whom, just that it's a possibility. Randy, being aware that his car *was* actually there, decides it's best not to deny it, believing he can cover it with a fabricated reason to justify his presence over on the north side of town.

R) "Erm, er yeah, I was giving one of the guys a ride home after we had drinks."

M) "That's nice of you, honey. Did you go for a couple in the Grand Hotel too?"

R) "Er, Yeah, I had a quick one in the hotel bar."

At this point Randy has admitted to being at the scene of the event and Maddison has had it undeniably confirmed by him that he was there.

M) "Is there any reason that somebody might have said that Chloe from your office was in the hotel bar too?"

Again, Maddison hasn't accused Randy of anything and also hasn't confirmed whether or not anyone has actually witnessed them being seen together, but in order to attempt to cover his tracks Randy has to assume that he's been seen.

R) Yeah, er she, er... well, she was at the hotel bar, yeah.

Now you have Randy and Chloe at the hotel bar together. Whereas before this point Randy would have totally denied the notion of he and Chloe being together, you now have them both placed at the hotel. You can see how this works so well for law enforcement officers in placing suspects at the scene of a crime. By allowing their own mind to work against them, you can steer the person down a path towards a full confession, step-by-step.

We will explore this in more depth later, but for now let's look at the possible outcomes of the above scenario.

M) "You told me you were drinking with Derek and Herb last night, right?"

R) "Yeah, why?"

M) "So, if I call them and ask them to tell me every venue that you were at last night, is there any reason they wouldn't mention the hotel?"

Randy is stuck here. Rather than confessing at this point to cheating on his wife with Chloe, he decides to dig himself in deeper in an attempt to cover the truth.

R) "I dropped them off first and was still in the mood for a quiet one, so I called into the hotel by myself for a quick drink."

Now you have Randy and Chloe drinking alone. He knew his friends wouldn't think to mention the hotel (because they weren't there), so he covered it another way. You are now a step closer.

With the variables of where the conversation could go from here being infinite, I'm just going to give you a guide on what could be used as the next approach, and we'll go into the exact method for extracting a confession shortly.

In this instance, though, the next steps could be to use the same approach to get Randy to confess to having a room, either by implying prior knowledge or asking him if you were to call the hotel would there be any reason they would say he had paid for a room, asking about receipts or booking confirmations etc. and so on.

The questions need to be kept light-mannered and non-confrontational. Being slow and precise allows the person being questioned enough time to think. This is highly important at this stage. If you fire off a burst of questions in rapid succession, then you don't give the person enough time to allow doubt to creep into their mind. The theory is simple; if it's kept nice and slow, not only can you monitor their response, but more importantly, they have enough time for a stream of guilty thoughts to enter their head. These thoughts are vital to the process of obtaining your confession. You need the person to truly believe certain parts of their story have been compromised and then allow them to try and explain the facts away. This will ultimately get you to force the person into admitting everything step by step.

We will cover the other signs to look for that signal deceit later, and how you go from lightly asking questions to getting the person to give a full confession as to their actions. This is the part where you make the transition from light questions to them telling you everything. It's a very delicate process that's so slight it's barely noticeable. But returning to my earlier point where I highlighted a person's desire to talk, if the transition is done correctly, this is what happens. You start with the questions, and they answer, until you slowly turn the tables, and now they are doing all the talking and you are only prompting (when necessary) what else you'd like them to tell you (more information on the right way to do that is coming up later too).

There are other factors at play that all make up part of the technique used to extract a confession. When all the elements are combined and utilized in a specific way, then the technique works like magic. As I mentioned earlier though, it is a very delicate process, and if it's not executed with care and precision then it could fall apart. As with most things in life, practice makes perfect.

This section will reveal questions you can ask that reveal guilt. Imagine a situation where a person is telling you that they got mugged on their way home. You're not sure why, but you get a gut feeling that they're lying. So you ask the following guilt-revealing question.

"How did that make you feel?"

A truthful person will know exactly how they felt at the time and will answer instantly with a response like "scared and vulnerable", or whatever their feeling would be. If it's not true however, they might answer with something different and possibly something like: "I don't know. Scared, I guess." That's when you know they're not telling the truth. Especially if you get the upward inflexion in the tone of their voice at the part they say, "I guess", making it sound more like a question than a statement. Truthful people know how they feel about something that happened. Only people who are lying need to ask or don't know how they feel about being mugged. Which, let's face it, is an emotional and traumatic event.

An extra snippet of useful information in this section is that it's easier to lie with a yes than a no. I know that might sound confusing at first, but for some reason, it seems that if you ask a person a question where the answer is yes, if they're lying, they find it less stressful to lie than if they had to answer with a no.

Let's look at a way a question can be rephrased to utilize this method. In the event of, say, a file being stolen from a filing cabinet you could ask:

"Was it there when you locked the filing cabinet up at the end of your shift yesterday?"

The person being questioned can easily answer with a yes because the question seems less accusatory. If you rephrase the question to:

"Did you take the file from the cabinet for any reason before you locked it up yesterday?"

They're then forced to answer in the negative. Asking a question that directly involves their participation to the missing file increases the burden of the question. We will explore this in more depth later on, but for now, we have established that they now need to answer with a no, and if they're lying, there's a higher chance of them showing it in their body language or response.

There are other questions that reveal guilt which we will explore in the section about obtaining a confession. They have the added advantage of confirming if a person is being truthful too. So you can be extra sure when it comes to your skills that you have got the whole truth and have not been deceived.

The Missing Link

Law enforcement officers use a clever technique when interviewing suspects called "Maybe I'm missing something". They might say something along the lines of:

"Maybe I'm missing something, but based on what you've said, it seems to me you actually wouldn't mind supplying the enemy with intelligence."

They then play the silence game. They deliberately say nothing and wait. This will cause an uncomfortable atmosphere, and the first to speak loses the game. Silence is extremely powerful. It's not usually long before the person being interrogated breaks out into a rapid succession of details. It seems so simple, yet you'd be surprised how many times the "maybe I'm missing something" line has been successful.

For now, though, we'll end this section and move onto body language.

4. B.L.B. Body Language Basics

During my career, I have travelled to many parts of the world, some very beautiful, some very interesting, and some I'd never want to return to again. One thing I've noticed, however, regardless of what part of the world I'm in, is I can usually get pretty much anything I need with a mixture of gestures and grunts. In areas popular for tourists, finding someone who speaks English isn't usually a major problem, but in some of the places I've travelled to just letting people know you're English isn't the wisest of options. So, again, pointing and making the right noises seemed to get me whatever I needed, with a bit of head nodding or shaking thrown in too.

People around the globe can pretty much gauge what you're after simply by the visual display of your physical actions, but is body language important in telling if someone is lying to you? The simple answer is yes. Although this isn't a body language book, it does indeed play a vital role in deception detection. Unlike many other books, I'm not only going to teach you the body language signals to look out for but ways to help you remember them too. That way you can implement them in your daily life until you reach a level of competence where it becomes natural to you.

In this section, we will cover the types of body language that might potentially show signs of deceit, but we will also cover several other body language signs too. The reason for this is so that you have an overall view of what to look for. Being able to spot if someone is being deceitful is one thing, but being able to spot if someone is being open and honest too is equally as useful. As we will discuss later, you will get what you look for, so it's important to be able to sign-count. One deceitful action that could possibly have been made in error by either party could result in conviction if you miss the ten other signs of being open and honest. So, in order to differentiate successfully between honesty and lies, you need to know the signs for both.

Being able to read people's body language over the years has proven to be invaluable to me on multiple occasions, but one thing we must get clear first is there are no absolutes. There's no single physical action that displays a lie. However, there are actions that can indicate a person's level of discomfort towards a given topic, question, or subject. This will then allow you to probe further, using techniques shown later in this book, to identify a lie or mistruth. Therefore, if you ask someone a question and they fold their arms, it does not mean they are going to lie, it doesn't even mean they're going into a defensive mode. It could mean they're not comfortable talking about that subject, maybe they're not comfortable talking about it in front of the present company, in the current situation or environment, or it could simply mean they wanted to fold their arms. Not every movement a person does signifies a feeling. However, there are certain actions, sometimes referred to as HPIs (High Percentage Indicators) that more often than not are a huge giveaway towards a person's true feelings or thoughts. These actions we'll explore in this section, which will assist you in finding the right areas to pursue in order to utilize the lie detection methods you'll learn later on.

Think about it like this: you want to find the lie, so using the signs and signals you're about to learn will show you which path to take in order to get you to the right area. Then, using the other techniques I'm going to teach you, you'll identify the lie and ultimately find the truth.

Why is it so hard to identify a lie? Well, aside from our inescapable biases, (which we will come back to) the truth is we're so good at it. Lying, that is. But why? Well, it's quite simple; We're all actually programmed to lie from a very young age. It's not a deliberate thing, but as small children we learn extremely fast.

Let me give you an example. As a toddler, I was playing in the kitchen and spilt a box of breakfast cereal all over the kitchen floor. In my mind I hadn't done anything wrong and continued to smear Lucky Charms all over the place by driving my matchbox cars through it all and crushing the contents of the now empty packet into a fine powder all around the kitchen. It was great fun. Not too long after, I ventured back into the living room to pull a different set of toys from the toy box and endeavored to make a new mess in another area of the house. In the meantime, my hard-working mother returned from pegging washing out onto the line to find my racetrack left abandoned in the kitchen. So, when she entered the living room and asked me, "did you pour all the Lucky Charms out onto the floor?" I simply replied, "yes", and the red handprint that was left on my hind taught me a valuable lesson. The problem was it taught me the wrong lesson. Instead of teaching me not to spill cereal everywhere, it taught me to lie next time I did it and blame my younger brother instead.

As funny as all this is, the same theory applies to the majority of people everywhere. It's a simple self-preservation theory (coming up: the only two reasons people lie). Plus, if we all told the truth all of the time, there would be a lot of seriously hurt feelings in the world to say the least. I'm sure I don't need to start with the "does my ass look fat in this?" examples. You probably have enough scenarios in your head without me adding more. The Jim Carrey film *Liar Liar* is a great example of how much trouble could be created if you were to say nothing other than the truth constantly. So, we've established that people lie a lot. In fact, according to Quora.com, on average, people lie around 200 times a day! About three times per every 10-minute conversation. While a 2002 study conducted by the University of Massachusetts found that 60% of adults can't have a 10-minute conversation without lying at least once.[1]

Here are some interesting facts when it comes to deception: from the age of six to seven months a baby learns to fake laughter. Between eight and nine months a child learns to wait until their parents are out of the room before attempting to do something they know they shouldn't. Between nine and 11 months a child learns to pretend not to hear when a parent is giving them an instruction they dislike. From 16 months a child learns to hide things, and at 18 months a child learns to hide themselves, usually to get out of doing something they dislike, or when they're playing and it's bedtime.

As we get older our intelligence levels increase, and our cognitive abilities improve. We simply get better and better at lying, especially

---

[1] mentalfloss.com/article/30609/60-people-cant-go-10-minutes-without-lying

if the reward from our lies pays off. It almost becomes a life skill as we grow.

As you can see, we've had a lot of practice, and lots of practice leads to becoming experts, whether that's intentional or not. Meaning we have become very, very good at lying. This is why it's so difficult to identify a lie. So, what does it take to beat an expert? Especially when that expert practices around 200 times a day. Well, by the time you've finished this book, although someone may well be an expert in lying, you'll be an expert in lie detection.

A major factor to take into consideration is that you need to look for what I call Groupings (sometimes known as clusters) of both body language and verbal signs to be able to identify possible deceit. I will expand on this later and demonstrate ways in which you will be able to put the methods into practice when it comes to registering these groupings and ticking them off as you go. With the ability to recognize the groupings of verbal and non-verbal signals, mixed with knowledge in other areas like tone, pitch, volume, speed, stance, expression, and more, you will be able to use these as signals of potential deception and implement the skills I will cover with you to ultimately get to the truth. It may sound a little daunting at the moment, but when you see how simple I will make it for you to learn each of these areas then put them all together, you will be more than satisfied with your new ability to read people better than you ever have been able to before. So, are you ready to begin?

Footloose

So, let's get into the meat and bones of it, shall we? We'll start with a revelation. If I were to ask you what part of the body reveals more about a person in the terms of body language, what would your answer be? Over the years I have heard a huge array of answers ranging from eyes, face, hands, or lips, but the shocking answer is in fact your feet! If you really want to know more about a person's mood, thoughts, frame of mind, or intentions then watch their feet. The TSA (Transportation Security Administration, an agency of the U.S. Department of Homeland Security) are trained to look at the direction of someone's feet at border control. If they are pointing straight towards the agent then it's a signal that all is well, however, if the body of the subject is facing the agent and the feet are turned away towards the exit, this is one of the main HPIs (High Percentage Indicators) that the person is uncomfortable, wanting to leave, or possibly has something to hide.

You can use this method another way too. If you are at a party, for example, and you approach two people talking, then watch their feet. If they keep their feet firmly planted facing each other then they wish to continue their conversation between only the two of them. In this instance ignore whatever their mouths say and listen to the language in which their body is talking. Excuse yourself and go and spike the punch instead. If they turned partly towards you, however, so all three of you look like you're standing on equal thirds of a pie, then that's their body language welcoming you in and asking you to join them.

So, what other signals do the feet send out? Well, you've heard the saying "head over heels in love", right? Well, it might sound crazy, but your feet can certainly indicate a lot about your true feelings towards another. For example, if you were to observe a couple on a date, if the pair have their feet almost touching, there is without a doubt a physical connection of attraction. The term "playing footsie" really does apply. New couples tend to play footsie under the table quite a lot as a form of flirtation. It also displays comfort with the other person as well as physical attraction.

Other ways feet display signs of attraction are through elevation. Think of the times in a cartoon when two characters kiss. During the kiss the characters seem to go up onto tip toes and sometimes in more exaggerated examples, one or both characters might literally float. Films in which the girl might stand on tiptoes, or even raise one leg during a kiss, provide more overstated examples of foot elevation. From a slightly different angle, have you ever seen a film where a police officer is standing up at the point of getting the upper hand on a criminal and momentarily lifts onto his tip toes and back down again? When children get excited looking at animals at the zoo, they tend to go up on tip toes. Most would think it's to get a better view, but the truth is it's simply excitement being displayed through foot elevation. Or what about this one? Have you ever been sitting with a pretty lady in high heel shoes, for an interview or meeting perhaps, and she crosses one leg and proceeds to dangle the shoe loosely from the end of her foot? Maybe even swaying it playfully? If that happens, believe me, you've got the job! And probably a couple of perks to go with it! This is another big sign of flirtation.

Foot elevation is a massive sign of happiness, excitement, flirtation, and of course, comfort. I'm sure you've heard the saying "put your feet up", right?

I suppose you could be thinking that all this is well and good but what does it have to do with lie detection? Well, as you are now aware of the signs being displayed for flirtation and comfort, we can discuss the signs displayed by the feet showing discomfort. According to Desmond Morris, the further away from the brain a body part is, the harder it is to control. Therefore, it stands to reason that the feet would be the most truthful and revealing part of the human body. So, what are the signs for deception, or more appropriately put; discomfort?

This sign is actually worked out quite easily. If a sign for comfort is moving your feet towards a person, then what do you think a sign for discomfort would be? Unsurprisingly, it's to move them away. I'll give you a very good example. I don't work in the field so much anymore, but I do still train operatives as well as the surveillance section for students on close protection courses with certain industry-leading companies. When I teach a class I have the layout arranged in a particular way. My preferred method is having the seats in a semi-circle facing the front of the training room as I teach. I do this deliberately so that I can watch the feet of the students. It's usually quite predictable; as the day starts, most of the class will have their feet either tightly under the front of the chair or tucked in as far back as they can get them under the seat. As the day progresses and the students become increasingly comfortable, their feet tend to stretch out further forward displaying a higher level of comfort. I will experiment with it sometimes too. If all the students seem reasonably comfortable with their legs stretched out and feet in front of them, I might watch their reaction as I tell the class it's time to test them and see if they were paying attention. Internally I'll begin to chuckle as I watch everyone sit up and all the feet tuck under the chairs again. Similarly, I might tell the group I'm going to pick someone at random to answer my next question. As I ask the question, I will closely watch the body language of the class, and if I see a student's feet shoot under the chair then I know this is an area they're not comfortable with and which might need further work for that student. For the record, I won't humiliate that particular student by picking them to answer the question if I know they're going to struggle with it. I will simply approach them in the break and offer help in that area, most of the time with a very surprised reaction and the student asking in amazement how I could possibly know that they were struggling with that section or topic. To which I generally reply with a smile; "it's my job".

Legging it

Sticking with our pattern of working form the ground up, we'll continue up the body from the feet to the next area, which is obviously the legs. I'm only going to skim over this quickly as it's predominantly related to the feet section. After all, they are joined together. So, with the legs, this is another area of reading the circumstance surrounding the actions. Just because someone has their legs crossed, for example, doesn't mean they're defensive or hiding something. On the other hand, even though having crossed legs isn't a definitive sign of discomfort, open legs are most certainly a sign of high levels of comfort, and more! There are way too many possible puns here, and I'm probably going to struggle to keep this clean. I've no doubt that at some point you've probably heard a conversation which included the phrase, "she opens her legs for any guy that smiles at her." Even though it might just be gossip based on rumors, the words themselves imply that people only open their legs to the people that they like. Now to stray away from the sexual innuendos, let's reframe the situation a little. Imagine a dad who's been working away, and as he stands in the street, a few yards in front of him his wife and young daughter spot him walking towards them. His daughter runs forward excitedly yelling "daddy, daddy". Naturally, he lowers himself to her level by bending his knees and opening his arms and legs to welcome her in and give her a hug. This open posture is an obvious sign of love, comfort, and trust. He has literally opened right up to welcome his daughter in. Not something anybody would dream of doing in a threatening or uncomfortable situation, obviously. Therefore, if a person chooses to sit with you in an open pose, then they are most certainly comfortable in your presence.

Going Nuts

Moving onwards and upwards. Quite literally, the next part of the body to be brought to your attention is the genitals. I know, open legs and genitals, whatever's coming next? In an attempt to move your mind in the right direction, I'll waste no time in stating that it's simply how a person presents themselves. Obviously, the genitals are an extremely vulnerable part of the body, so if the genitals are closely guarded, like in the situation of a person's legs being crossed, then this could be a sign of a defensive posture. I use the word *could* simply because, As I said earlier, it may also be merely that the person wants to sit with their legs crossed. This is an area you have to be careful not to misread. It stands to reason that if a person is comfortable and doesn't feel the need to guard their genitals, they might stand or sit with an open posture. If a person feels threatened or uncomfortable, though, there is a very high chance they will stand or sit in a way that keeps their genitals protected.

While we're in the groin area, I'm going to talk about an action performed more by men than women. This is slightly contradictory to other parts of the book, but when a male becomes both confident and defiant, they are more likely to sit with an open crotch, displaying their genital area. Psychologists say this form of body language actually raises testosterone and lowers cortisol. This is a man's body language shouting out that he's feeling cocky! It displays extremely high levels of confidence bordering on arrogance, as well as comfort, and even rebelliousness.

On the flipside, the guarding of the genitals is a sure sign of high levels of discomfort. Once, in a certain situation, I was forced into becoming confrontational with a particular man, and when I showed signs of aggression, he put his hands with his palms facing out in front in an attempt to keep a gap between us, but he also bent his body in such a fashion that his butt was sticking out behind him. It wasn't because he wanted to stick his ass out on display, but rather to guard his family jewels. As I yelled at him, he took tiny little steps backwards to move his genitals further away but kept the top half of his body where it was, looking like he was part way through bending over. This action is performed when feeling threatened and is another natural response.

Thus, in order to gauge a person's level of comfort, look at their crotch area (look, don't stare!). It will either be guarded, natural, or openly displayed most of the time and will give you a pretty accurate indication of how they're feeling in that moment.

Stacking Things Up

There are ways in which the torso can give you a clue as to a person's thoughts and feelings too. A few years ago, I was hired by a high-status couple who were concerned about their 24-year-old daughter, who kept insisting she had a stalker who was causing her to live in fear. The couple worked away frequently, and their daughter was home alone the majority of the time. Yet again, I'm not going to reveal the true name of the girl in question, but for the ease of explanation, I'll refer to her as Gina. I took on the temporary task of Residential Security at Gina's house, and all seemed to be going well during the course of week one. She didn't seem to be the spoilt little rich girl I was anticipating, but rather a well-mannered 24-year-old who was pretty switched on. Even though Gina seemed a tad jumpy from time to time, I performed the regular checks, carried out my duties and the first week went by with no signs of a stalker.

At the start of week two I had gotten to know Gina reasonably well (while remaining at a professional distance), and we would sit and have friendly chats most days. It wasn't until the start of week three that something unusual happened. We were sat on the sofa in the family room one evening, a couple of hours before her normal bedtime, and she randomly asked if I'd ever shot anyone. Which seemed a very unusual question and also ostensibly seemed to come out of nowhere. I replied with, "yes, why do you ask?" to which she dismissively said, "Oh, I just wondered."

Now, you don't have to have a degree in psychology to know that her dismissive statement was response bait. So I played along, knowing she wanted me to pursue. That way it looks like I coaxed it out of her, and she can justify not simply blurting information out. So I continued.

It seemed she wanted to know if I'd shoot her stalker if he broke into the house. Even though it appeared a rational desire for a sense of security, something seemed off with her body language. I couldn't quite put my finger on it, so I decided to probe a little. I continued with the conversation and began to ask a few more details about the stalker. Then, little alarm bells started to ring inside my head. My line of questioning became more specific. In a very casual and non-aggressive manner, I asked how many times she'd actually seen him, what he was wearing, and how she could be sure it was definitely the same person. I then detected a couple of patterns.

When I showed support towards her predicament, her body language was very open, but when I quizzed her about the specifics of her stalker, she would pull her feet up onto the sofa. Then a few more tell-tale signs emerged when I enquired more about the man in question. She started to pull the scatter cushions up from around her, hugging the first one into her tummy area. Now this is one of the HPIs that a person is uncomfortable. Which, when talking about a stalker, is highly understandable, so the big picture eluded me for a while before I finally put the pieces together.

I decided to approach from a different angle, and that's when the truth came out. It wasn't the talking about her stalker that made her uncomfortable. What was making her uncomfortable was the fact that I might find out that she had made the whole thing up. Her simple plan for an attention cry had spiraled out of control a little. She had no choice but to continue with it, even to the extreme of letting her parents hire a Close Protection Operative to live in their house with her while they were away. The crazy thing is I hadn't initially noticed that during the course of the conversation she had gone to the extreme of piling up all of the scatter cushions around her until just her head and shoulders were peeking out of the top of her mini cushion fortress. I still to this day don't know exactly how far she would have gone with it, and I'm glad I never got the chance to find out. Who knows, she could have arranged for some guy to call around the house late one night in the hopes I might have shot the intruder. An innocent party that she could have claimed was her stalker. Let's face it, if a beautiful girl asked a young college lad to come around her house that night and climb in through the window on a promise, there aren't that many who would refuse. I'm glad it never got that far.

In conclusion, the guarding of her torso with the cushion was a signal of discomfort, and people will tend to put barriers in front of them when they feel uncomfortable with a situation. This action is a subconscious way of guarding oneself. When there are no physical objects to place in front of the body, this is when the arms or legs can come into play.

There is also a reversal of this situation I'd like to address here too. I was at a small business on the south coast of England when a man walked in and demanded to speak to the owner. When the owner emerged (a huge fellow that looked like he should be green and standing in a cornfield), the man that had walked in launched into an offensive verbal attack, shouting how he'd been more than patient and wanted some money he was owed.

The owner looked slightly stunned and a little concerned and tried to pacify the man but to no avail. The man had clearly had enough and wanted payment. Then, something happened that surprised me. Instead of placing objects in the way on the counter between them, the owner started to move things out of the way. I was a little confused to say the least. I'd seen people put objects in place as a barrier when feeling threatened before, but never moving them out of the way. My initial thought was maybe the owner was preparing to jump the counter and fight with the man shouting at him. As it happened, the situation calmed a little, and they talked through their differences before it got out of hand. I thought about it for a little time and it bugged me, even though it was my belief that he was possibly clearing the counter ready to leap over and fight, something didn't quite add up and I felt I was missing something.

That night I got my answer. Not because I worked it out for myself but because I got in touch with an expert that I have huge admiration for and who, in my opinion, is one of the best in the world when it comes to reading people. Not only is he a body language expert but an expert in reading people in general. A former army interrogator and amazing individual, Greg Hartley.

I cannot sing the praises of this man enough. We spoke on the phone for a while, and Greg deduced that the reason the business owner was moving things around on the counter was not in preparation to jump it, but in fact it was something much simpler. It was control. As the boss, surrounded by all his staff who were watching him being belittled, he had to do something. So he moved items around on the counter in an attempt to demonstrate a little control where he actually had none.

Greg is a great guy and I highly recommend his books as well as his course and membership site. He is a partner of Scott Rouse, yet another amazing man and phenomenal expert in human behavior. They both make up half of *The Behaviour Panel*, which in my opinion is the best body language channel on YouTube, along with Chase Hughes (whom I mentioned earlier), and last but certainly not least, Mark Bowden (voted the world's number one body language expert). If you haven't already, go and check out their channel. You can thank me later.

Before we finish this section on the body, I'd like to point out that to almost every rule there is an exception. The guarding of the chest in a defensive display of behavior is not to be confused with other times when a person might have their hands or arms in front of their chest. Blocking their chest with their arms can be considered a defensive movement, but just imagine a situation where you give someone a beautiful gift that they love. This particular hands-to-the-heart motion is actually a sign of sincerity and obviously not a defensive posture. It all comes down to the circumstances. So as with everything, when it comes to deception detection, dynamic assessment is key. One action might mean something completely different in another set of circumstances. This is why there's no body language dictionary, like I said earlier. It comes down to reading the individual and the situation. Only then can you come up with a more accurate reading of the person's thoughts or intentions.

The Cold Shoulder

This one ties in neatly with congruency (which we covered earlier). If the shrugging of the shoulders is congruent with what is being said, then everything is as it should be. For example: A person might shrug their shoulders when saying something like, "I don't know anything about quantum physics." If they genuinely don't know anything about quantum physics and shrug as they say it, then that is body language that's congruent with what's being said.

If, however, they say something like, "I've never accessed your files." This body language is not congruent with what's being said. You shrug when you don't know something, not when you haven't done something. This also applies to spoken words, not just to actions.

For example, the utterance "I don't know what the doctor said" when accompanied by a shoulder shrug is congruent. Whereas "I didn't say anything to her about you" with a shoulder shrug, is not. Is this a definitive sign of deceit? In a word, no. It is, however, a really high percentage indicator of something that needs investigating further. Using the new knowledge that you will have gained from the rest of this book to read further into what the person is saying, along with a little further questioning, you will be able to find out what that might be.

As with every rule, there is always an exception, and this is where you will have to rely on the other skills you will learn to differentiate between if what you're seeing is deception or if it's congruent with what's being said. An example of a person not caring about a particular event, for instance, they may shrug their shoulders as they say something like, "I don't care if the bus comes or not. If it doesn't, I'll get an Uber." Or, "I don't care what Sharon said about me, I don't let these things bother me." In these examples, a shoulder shrug is acceptable and more than likely congruent too. You will have to decide for yourself using other methods I will teach you later on if they really do care about what Sharon said about them, or if they would actually rather take the bus or the Uber.

I also think I should mention here that a slight one-sided shoulder shrug is just as significant, if not more of a signal, than both shoulders being shrugged at the same time. It's usually very slight and harder to spot but with practice can be observed and taken into account. The one-sided shoulder shrug is also more common, especially with deception, or if a person has a lack of belief in what they are saying.

Another time the shoulders come into play, is when a person is 'Turtle-necking' (body language terminology for when their head seems to come down and their shoulders come in and up slightly, like that of a turtle's head retracting into its shell). Turtle-necking usually signifies a lack of confidence, possible insecurity, and usually being uncomfortable. It's definitely one to look out for when it comes to deception. Alone (as with almost any single action when it comes to body language) it doesn't mean too much, but with a group of other tells, it can definitely indicate possible deception.

Lastly when it comes to shoulders, with regards to body language, look for the dominant shoulder moving back slightly when saying or listening to a particular sentence. This is a strong indication that they do not agree with what is being said. Once again, it takes a little practice, but with all the lessons in this book, the more you do something the better you become.

Putting Your Neck on the Line

Moving up past the chest area, the next part of the body is the neck. Once again, a vulnerable area, especially the throat which is vital to survival. Blocking the throat can most certainly be a signal of deception. For example, Some time ago I was dating a girl called Lexi. A very attractive girl with long glossy black hair who wouldn't have looked out of place on an episode of *The Kardashians*. After our first date, we went back to my place and after a couple of glasses of wine, she spent the night there. The following morning, we got up and I took her for breakfast. (Hint for the guys here: if you take a girl home and can't remember her name in the morning, then take her to Starbucks. Give her the money to pay while you use the restroom. When the barista brings the coffees out and shouts your name and the name of the girl you're with, bingo!) Anyway, we're sitting having breakfast, and I asked Lexi how long she'd been single. Her answer was evasive, saying something like, "Oh for a while now, I'm not sure exactly."

Now, if there's one thing I know for certain about the opposite sex, it's that when it comes to times and dates, they're a walking calendar. That was only a small red flag though, because she may have simply been embarrassed with revealing the exact length of time. What really grabbed my attention is when I asked how come things ended with her previous boyfriend, she began to twiddle with the pendant on the end of her necklace. Sliding it left and right along the links of the chain. Ultimately enabling her to keep her hand in front of her throat area. I didn't push too much, as she was clearly not comfortable with talking about her previous relationship.

On the next date she came over to mine again, and we sat watching a movie with a bottle of wine and an array of snacks. Now over the years I've worked with myriad different people and have heard all sorts of stories, as well as experienced situations, where undercover officers from MI5, KGB, CIA, FBI, and other organizations have deliberately put themselves in situations where they have a high probability of being caught. Maybe by taking unnecessary risks like carrying their own ID instead of that of their legend (their Legend being the alias they're using whilst undercover). Even leaving their wallet lying around with both sets of ID inside the same wallet, and in some extreme cases, even their warrant card or government ID.

The reason for this is simple. Deep down everybody knows lying is wrong and can't help but to feel guilty about deceiving people, even if it is for a greater good in the long term. So as an undercover agent, operative, or officer gets closer to their target, they have been known to develop an attachment (in some instances even fall in love) or become extremely close friends with their subject. The self-sabotage actions of taking risks with a possibility of being caught are due to feelings of guilt and the subconscious desire to be punished for their deception.

What's this got to do with you burning calories with Lexi? I hear you ask. Well after a few dates I could sense something wasn't quite as it should be. Even though I couldn't put my finger on it straight away, there was definitely something not right. The first couple of weeks we spent a fair amount of time together, but suddenly it was harder to get her to commit to a specific time or day, and she would just randomly show up at mine late at night to stay over. I decided to get to the bottom of it, we sat down in the front room and I began asking a few specific questions. It wasn't long before she revealed that she had a boyfriend! When she had first met me, he was in Vegas on a 2-week stag holiday, and while he was enjoying time on the roulette table, she was enjoying time on me. She insisted that it had never meant to go any further, but she couldn't help herself and wanted to carry on seeing me. Needless to say, even as pretty as she was, I ended the relationship once and for all… the next morning!

The whole trigger for my suspicion, though, was brought about by her simply twiddling with her necklace pendant. Other signs a person might be uncomfortable with the conversation or possibly being deceitful include tugging at their shirt collar with their index finger or, one of the most common, rubbing their hand around the back of their neck. Like they're giving themselves a partial massage. The way I remember this tell is simply thinking of the term "pain in the neck". If a person makes this action, then their thoughts are this person/subject/situation is a pain in the neck. It would certainly raise suspicion with me if a person did this upon a particular subject that's been brought up.

In a different situation, the exposing of the neck can show physical attraction. I took a girl on a date once, and not long after we got there, she pulled her hair off her neck and tilted her head slightly. I'm not going to bore you with the science behind why it happens, but basically if a woman finds you attractive her body temperature rises as she gets aroused. This is why moving the hair away from her neck sends a signal that's twofold. The first thing is that the temperature rise is making her sweat a little, and so removal of the hair is helping her to stop overheating. The second is that the exposed neck with the head tilt shows a vulnerability and that she's comfortable with you. So comfortable she can expose an area that would be closely guarded otherwise. While on this topic, I want to clear something up here. Just because a woman moves her hair away from her neck doesn't necessarily mean she's attracted to you, look for several indicators. Look to see if her feet are close to yours. Look to see if there's prolonged eye contact and her blink rate slows. See if she makes frequent physical contact, even the slightest of touches can show her levels of comfort with you. There are more which we can go into later, but I feel I must stress that the common saying that a woman plays with her hair when she's attracted to you needs to be addressed here. If you want to know the truth, ask yourself this: when does a woman play with her hair? Answer: All the time! Yes, all the time. Ladies are almost constantly playing with their hair, and it can be easy to go down a path of misreading signs of flirtation if you think she's attracted to you just because she plays with her hair.

A quick hint to look more confident here is to stand up straight and keep your neck extended when talking on webcams and during online meetings etc. It's easy to try and get a good camera angle in an attempt to show your best side, but a lot of people do this and end up inadvertently making the head look closer to the shoulders. This shows signs that would make people think you're untrustworthy and could create issues for you. You may not get chosen for a particular role, or worse. Instead, set your webcam up so you're sat or standing up straight, with your neck extended and a soldier-like posture: chin up, shoulders back. There's no need to go over the top with this; you don't want to look like you're trying to impersonate the school bully or that you're trying to pass yourself off as aggressive. Just an upright posture is enough.

Up In Arms

Next, I'm going to cover the arms. Our arms are our natural shields: our first line of defense in an attack and our instinctive way of blocking incoming threats. You've only got to look at sports like boxing for a couple of minutes to see how effective our arms are at being our best form of physical protection. Therefore, it stands to reason that when a person feels threatened, their immediate and sometimes subconscious response is to shield their body with their arms defensively. In a physical situation when an altercation is highly possible (like the situation I mentioned earlier), a person might put both their arms out in front of them, palms facing out, attempting to keep distance between themselves and their assailant, thus guarding the body's vital organs. In the instance that a person is being questioned, though, they would look rather daft if they performed that same action, so instead they might find another way of bringing their arms in front of them. An example would be, yes you guessed it, folding their arms. Now I hate to talk about this particular action purely because of the stigma attached to it, and the myth that has been circulating for years that folded arms indicate you're telling a lie or being defensive. That's simply not the case. I fold my arms all the time. I personally find it an extremely comfortable position for me, as I'm sure many other people do too.

As I said at the beginning of this book, there is no single definitive action that the body can make to indicate 100% accurately if a person is lying or not. There are only indicators of a person's level of discomfort with a situation or topic. It is down to you to first establish a baseline of whether this is a normal action for this person to take or not, and then to dynamically assess whether you should pursue a particular line of questioning to get to the truth. I will cover more methods of revealing the lie itself later, so that you can combine them all for an accurate assessment of whether someone is being truthful or not, as well as how to extract a confession if they are lying. Back to the arms though. Does folding your arms mean you're being defensive? The answer is both yes and no. It can, in a situation when it's not a normal action for a person, or how that person normally sits or stands. At the same time, it might not be, if that person frequently has their arms folded. It's a judgement call at best.

When it comes to the arms guarding the body, like the phrase from the Farm, it depends. You have to take the whole situation into account and decide if the action is warranted, such as if they were clock watching and wanted to check the time on their wristwatch due to an upcoming appointment, or if they simply moved their arms in front of them when a particular topic was mentioned.

As with everything, just keep your eye out for what's not normal for that person. Just as we covered earlier, you can now see how the importance of establishing a baseline is coming into play.

Hands Up

Let's carry on, then, with body language signals that are more accurate when it comes to revealing a person's state of mind, moving down the arms to the hands and how they can reveal a lot more than you think. I'm going to split this into two sections with the shorter part first. Hands can reveal a lot about a person's frame of mind. Not just with how they display them but also with touch. Without going overboard on the personal space theory, it's pretty unlikely that a person would frequently make physical contact with another in a standard social gathering. A handshake or pat on the back is about the usual limit. So as I said earlier, if you find yourself conversing with a beautiful lady who's frequently touching you, then this is a surefire sign of flirtation. She might jokingly push you or be finding excuses to rub your arm, even if it's hidden in subtle guises of liking the feel of your shirt or some other excuse. This has been the case for years, and recently I've been working with a couple of young women who have openly confirmed that this is still the case, even amongst the younger generation. Of course, I disguised the reason of my questioning in another form. As a former MI6 colleague of mine once said, "if in doubt, pretend you're stupid!" And it's served me well over the years. People tend to say a lot more if they think you're stupid! Back to the topic though, a woman's hands can certainly reveal her feelings towards you. Regular touching is a definitive sign of attraction, unless of course her hands are regularly touching you by gripping you around the neck and squeezing your throat!

Another way that the hands can give away a person's feelings is when they make a rubbing action on another part of the body. For example, if a person is sitting down and they begin to rub their thighs with their hands or make a brushing action with their hands on the tops of their legs, this is a pacifying behavior. I was torn between putting this into the legs section or the hands section because I suppose, really, it's both. But sweeping the tops of your thighs with the palms of your hands is a sign of self-comforting. And of course, you would only self-comfort at such a time when you feel uncomfortable. So, if you're chatting away and a person starts rubbing the tops of their legs then you can take it as a nonverbal statement that the person is uncomfortable with the situation or topic. To go a step further, if a person becomes extremely uncomfortable with what's unfolding, they may go to the extremes of hiding their hands. Possibly tucking them underneath their legs, so they're sitting on their own hands or even folding their arms and tucking them into an area where they will be unseen or covered by a jacket or clothing item. On the flipside, a confident person will have their hands on display. Someone who is exceptionally confident might even steeple and spread open their fingers in front of them, regardless of whether they're standing or sitting.

Penultimately, in this section we come to the thumbs. Tucking of the thumbs into pockets or just generally hiding them from sight is yet another tell-tale sign of a lack of confidence, or a feeling of uncomfortableness. Probably one of the reasons why the military drill it into soldiers to keep their hands out of their pockets. If you watch a group of people in almost any setting, the one with their hands in their pockets is the one right down the bottom of the pecking order.

Finally, I'm going to give you a HPI that is one of the most accurate signals that a person is being deceitful or hiding the truth. As I said earlier, unlike in the United States you don't need a license to be a private investigator in the UK. So pretty much anyone can set up shop and start running their own private investigations company. Becoming established, though, is a different story altogether. Like I used to say to some of my clients, if you think hiring a professional is expensive, wait until you hire an amateur! Before I moved up the ladder into the intelligence community I started at the very bottom.

Over the years I've noticed that most people in the UK seem to think that the only way to be an Intelligence Officer is to work for MI5, MI6, or GCHQ. That's simply not the case. There are many government departments that have Intelligence Officers, not just those three. Even the UK's Environment Agency has its own Intelligence Officers. An even bigger revelation to a lot of people is that there are also many private intelligence companies too. 5 Stones Intelligence and Athena Intelligence are just a couple of the main ones in England. Just like private military companies (frequently hired by the government), the private intelligence companies operate in a similar way. It should go without saying of course that freelance contractors are hired frequently, especially if they're recommended.

After many years of working freelance in the industry, I still get approached from time to time, even though I seldom work in the field anymore. On this particular occasion, I was approached by a man from a growing private intelligence company with quite a pitch. I won't tell you the man's real name, so let's call him Barry. He arranged a meeting with me which included a lavish meal in a top

London hotel, and his proposal sounded incredibly good. He was confident and excited about where it all could lead for me, and the deal seemed tempting. Barry's body language all the way through his offer showed all the usual signs of confidence, and the more he talked his way through his proposition, the more confidence both his vocals and his body displayed. Something changed, however, when he finished his pitch and asked me if I had any questions. As great as his offer sounded, I did actually have a few questions. Even though he replied with the right words, when he was answering some of the more difficult parts of my questions, he was making a wringing action with his hands. Kind of like he was washing his hands without any soap or water.

Now this action can also be made by someone who's excited, but because he'd not done it at any other point earlier on in the meeting, and I'd previously established a baseline of his normal actions when he was in conversation, I knew this was an indication of his discomfort with certain questions, and that he wasn't being entirely honest. I didn't say anything at the time (which is nothing new for me), but I waited for his email outlining the agreed terms of his proposal to be put in the form of a contract, and it was very different to the terms he'd agreed in the meeting. Not only that, but the specific areas I'd asked about were definitely not as Barry had verbally informed me they were. Needless to say, I politely declined the offer and didn't even bother to waste my time or theirs trying to negotiate.

In summary, though, had I not spotted Barry's action of wringing his hands at delicate points of my questioning, I may not have paid as much close attention to those areas where I thought he wasn't being entirely truthful and just gone ahead and agreed to the terms of the contract. Once again, the wringing of the hands is not an action that can be considered a foolproof display of deceit; it was only the fact that this was abnormal behavior for Barry that alerted me to his holding back on the truth. Incidentally, it all worked out for the best for me because the firm dissolved less than 12 months later. Lucky escape.

Before we move on, the general rule when it comes to hands is as follows: if you can see them, that's a good thing, and if you can't, it's not, but like I said, take everything into account, including the temperature or weather. Most of the time, palms on display are a show of openness, or in some cases a defensive posture. In the instances of trying to calm a situation, palms up is considered a non-aggressive stance.

Going as far as we can, we're going to cover fingers next. I'll keep this really simple: watch a person's hands carefully as you talk. If their fingers are relaxed, then so are they. If they start to curl, then the tension is building. The more they curl, the more the tension within them builds. If you get to the point where they have clenched fists, then you may have pushed them too far. It doesn't need to result in aggression though. A small gesture of the fingers curling in at the mention of a particular subject can be enough to identify a negative association with that subject and should prompt you to probe further.

Another thing to look for is when a person has folded arms and their fingers are wrapped around their upper arm. If the fingers tighten around their arm, this is yet another sign of tension growing. Just like on a flat surface such as a tabletop, only this time the action is happening vertically instead of horizontally. In short, the fingers curling is a signal you should be looking for no matter where the hand is located.

Facing the Truth

Well, we've worked our way up the body to the neck, so obviously the head is next. I'm going to kick off with a simple pacifying behavior, namely using the back of your hand or fingers to rub your cheeks. If I had to guess, I would say this would originate from when a parent uses the back of their fingers to adoringly stroke the cheeks of a newborn baby. The cute baby feels loved by the parent who is soothingly stroking their cheeks with affection, and thus this results in the action of that person stroking their cheeks to pacify themselves later on in life. There's no scientific proof of this anywhere, it's simply my own opinion of where this action could have originated. I have seen it several times when a person wants to calm themselves. Another sign of a person attempting to pacify themselves or relieve stress is the puffing up of the cheeks followed by a long exhale. This blowing action is often seen just after a near miss or close call of some kind.

Imagine somebody just avoiding an accident then puffing up their cheeks and blowing out long and hard with relief. Similarly, the puffing up of the cheeks followed by the blowing out in the process of answering a question is also a HPI that someone is not being entirely truthful or is uncomfortable with the subject etc. Think of it like this, they are physically holding the question back until the words eventually escape on the exhale. This is usually a good sign that the person is possibly stressed by the question or subject, and their answer might not be entirely truthful.

Moving on but working in the same area, we're going to study the lips. This area can be huge when it comes to giving HPIs. At a time of concern, stress, or anxiety the lips tend to become compressed. When I was undergoing my defensive driver training, I was first given an eye-opening drive by the instructor to demonstrate his skills. I can assure you that in my first ride in the car with him, my pulse was pounding. MI5 are taught to drive by advanced police driving instructors who show them how to maneuver tactically at high speed through busy traffic and built-up areas without the use of flashing lights and sirens. It might surprise you to find out that MI5 officers don't have hidden blue lights in their vehicles for emergencies. They simply rely on their skills when it comes to driving. At the end of their driver training, they have to complete a test which involves driving from London to Scotland at speeds of over 130 mph in the safest, yet quickest, way possible, all the time giving a constant verbal account of the process to the examiner. So, believe me when I say that the skills of the instructor that taught me were second to none and had my adrenalin rushing.

Why is this relevant, I hear you ask? Well, have you ever been a passenger in a car driven at high speed? I'm sure you have at some point. What about a vehicle driven dangerously? I know from when I have experienced it, I've involuntarily pressed my leg down hard on the floor, like I was pressing an imaginary brake pedal. It's not there. We all know it's not there, but for some reason people tend to do it anyway. Maybe this in itself is some form of pacifying behavior. The point is though, certain circumstances can make your body react in certain ways. Just like when at high speeds your foot presses against the floor, when a person is anxious about a subject or withholding an opinion on that subject, they will tend to press their lips together.

Smiles themselves can also be a giveaway on a person's true feelings. A simple way to spot if a smile is genuine or not is to look at the eyes. If the mouth shows a smile but the person's eyes have not moved, it is a false smile. A real smile forces the corners of the mouth up towards the eyes, whereas a fake smile makes the corners of the mouth move towards the ears, and there is little emotion displayed in the eyes.

Puckering or pursing of the lips is also a HPI that a person's thoughts are in disagreement with what is being said, or that they are thinking of a possible alternative. Lip-pursing can be seen frequently during police interviews. A suspect might purse their lips in disagreement because they know the investigator has their facts wrong. It is also something that law enforcement officers look for when presenting incorrect evidence, a tactic used frequently by the police.

For example, I recently advised an individual on a case he was being investigated for in which I knew he was innocent. Once again, I'm not going to reveal the person's identity or the nature of the alleged crime, but for the sake of this book let's call him Phillip. Now Phillip was taken to the police station to be interviewed where they told him they had 262 photographic images sent by him to a third party committing a crime. It wasn't true, so why did they say it? Well, simply put, most people in this situation would start yelling out something like: "No way! You're so wrong I only sent 4 photos!" not realizing that instead of making the police look like idiots for getting their facts wrong, they've just made themselves the idiot by admitting to sending 4 photos and ultimately the crime. In this instance, Phillip pursed his lips when presented with the incorrect information and simply let out a small sarcastic laugh when he answered, "no comment." as advised. This indicated to the interviewer that even though Phillip answered with "no comment", he was fully aware that they had no such evidence; they were presenting him with incorrect information. A good interviewer would have picked up on the pursed lips alone and not needed the little chuckle from Philip confirming he knew full well that they did not in fact have the images they said they had. Some people also move their pursed lips side to side as they think.

Licking of the lips is another sign of nervousness. It might not mean a person is lying but it is another pacifying action. Not to be confused with times it's used for flirtation of course. An old trick I was taught years ago to get a girl to kiss you is to use the triangle method. Imagine talking to a girl and making the shape of an upside-down isosceles triangle between her eyes and her mouth, her two eyes being the corners of the triangle and her mouth being the point of the triangle. To begin with, eye contact is paramount. Stand front on to her, and as you converse with her, move your eyes up and down the triangle. From her eyes to her lips and back repeatedly. Not too quickly or you might look like you're having some kind of a fit. Just slowly and subtly. As you do this, subtly lick your lips and continue to actively listen to what she is saying. It won't be too long before you are both kissing, or she's at least thinking about kissing you. You'll find if she's thinking about it, then sooner or later it will be happening. Obviously, it helps to build a little sexual tension first, but that's for another book!

Covering of the lips with your fingers can be another sign of mistruth. I always tend to think that if the person is blocking their mouth with their hands or fingers like they're trying to hold the words back from coming out, simply because of the subconscious desire not to lie. So, by placing a finger or fingers in front of the mouth, they are attempting to form a barrier against the words from escaping.

In fact, any movement that serves to cover the lips in any way should be a red flag. Whether it's with a finger, a full hand, a book, or some other item, or even scratching the nose. Yes, the scratching of the nose, even though it's a different area of the face, still requires the lips to be covered by the hand. You could even be scratching the forehead and the arm covers the mouth, so look out for that kind of action. Remember here that this is only one sign and one sign alone is not enough to know for sure if someone is being deceitful. There could be a good reason for it but we'll cover that later.

Moving up from the lips to the nose, I think you'll find, this an easy area to get to know. We crinkle our nose naturally at things we don't like. For example, think of the face we make when we detect a bad smell. That crinkled up nose motion can be given in a fleeting moment to indicate disgust, dislike, or disapproval. If you make a suggestion, and the person you are talking to makes that crinkled nose expression for a fraction of a second, then they are not in agreeance.

There is another way the nose can indicate deceit too, and no, it doesn't grow when you tell lies! An interesting fact you may not be aware of is that there is actually erectile tissue in the nose and blood rushes to your nose when you become stimulated. With the rush of adrenalin, the human body goes into fight or flight mode, and this erectile tissue creates a sensation and might cause a person to scratch or rub their nose repeatedly. I do need to stress here, though, that this reaction can be caused by nervousness and isn't a definitive sign that a person is being deceitful. Once again, it comes down to reading the situation and taking all the details into account. I know I have mentioned this several times, but I believe it's imperative to keeping everything in perspective.

Even though we have covered other parts of the face, I have decided the eyes are such a great way of spotting deceit that they are going to have an entire section devoted to themselves, and the ways eyes reveal deceit will be covered later on in this book. So for now, we will move on, but we will definitely be coming back to cover the eyes later on, and believe me, it's a great section that will teach you so much when it comes to deception detection.

Head On

In the same way that the nose crinkles to display distaste or disapproval, the crinkling of the forehead is an easy way to spot discomfort or anxiety. Whilst talking about the forehead, look to see which way it's pointing. If it is facing up, this is a display of confidence. Think of the way members of royalty walk, nose in the air and forehead pointing up, extremely confident as they make strides. Now think of the opposite, a person looking down as they walk. This displays low confidence, or possibly concern. Watch carefully, and it's almost like they're trying to tuck their chin into their neck.

An extra little bit of information is turning your head to the right makes you look more attractive, and tilting your head to the left makes you look more intelligent. Although I wouldn't do them both at the same time as I think you'd more than likely have the opposite effect in both instances.

Another way the head can reveal a person's true thoughts is by giving slight shaking movements when answering yes to a question, or slight nods when answering no. You might think that you'd notice such an action, or that it's too obvious, but I've seen it happen more frequently than you might think. Only a couple of days ago I watched two people conversing, and when the girl asked the guy she was talking to if he'd received her message, he replied with "no", yet nodded yes with his head. It was so slight it was barely noticeable, but I knew instantly that he wasn't being truthful. Of course, this can easily be misread if someone is answering a question where they respond "yes, of course I did", while shaking their head slowly from side to side. This can be an indication of disbelief of the question or the situation. You need more than this one signal alone to know if someone is being deceitful.

Micro-expressions

Intelligence officers and caseworkers frequently use social engineering and NLP (Neuro Linguistic Programming) to assist them in recruiting new assets or sources. To fully explain NLP is a little difficult, as it's a tree with many branches. The easiest way to describe it overall, is a form of mind control. Now I know that might sound a little freaky, but it's not quite what you may first think. It's a bit like a cross between hypnosis and sales pitch. Kind of like a way to convince a person using particular ques, or "Anchors", as they are officially called by NLP Practitioners.

Personally, I'm a qualified hypnotist and NLP practitioner. Some people may be skeptical about the subject, but there's no getting away from the fact that the mind is a very powerful entity, and if it can be accessed correctly then it can also be utilized accordingly.

Let me explain a little more about NLP. I'm going to start with something called "anchors" first. For no other reason than this was the order I was taught in. Setting an Anchor is a form of conditioning. You can 'set' an anchor in a person in several ways. One of the easiest ways to explain how and why you would want to is this: Let's assume you want your wife to go to your parents' house for the weekend, but you know she's not going to be happy about it. If you could set a 'positive anchor', then you simply 'fire' this positive anchor at the point of asking the question. This will trigger a good feeling about going to see your parents at the weekend and, ultimately, she will agree, even though she hates your mom. So how do you set a positive anchor? Well, there are several ways to set an anchor that might be physical, audible or visual. To start things off, let's begin with setting a physical anchor. Every time your wife is in a really good mood, feeling good, gets good news, laughs, or you hand her a surprise present that you know will make her feel elated, simply touch her right elbow.

It works in a way very similar to Pavlov and his dogs. Pavlov used to ring a bell every time he set food down for his dogs. After a certain period of time, they associated the bell with feeding time and would salivate at the sound of the bell and the anticipation of food being placed down for them. Eventually, Pavlov could ring the bell and the dogs would salivate without the food, due to the association of bell ringing with feeding time. This is one example of an audible anchor. In the same way, your wife will associate being touched on the right elbow with a positive feeling, so when you ask a question and are touching the right elbow at the time, the association will trigger a good feeling and she is more likely to comply with your request.

The elbow is suggested as the best area for a few reasons. For one, it's easy to access without too much trouble. Another is that it can hardly be considered inappropriate, but most importantly, it's a vulnerable area (like most joints on the body). Even though the conscious mind might dismiss it, the subconscious mind will be very aware of the physical contact in that area, while simultaneously being aware of the mood or feelings in the subject at the time of being touched in that area too.

Positive anchors can simply put you in a good mood and give you a really good feeling. Think of it like this: do you know a song that, when it's played, just puts you in a really good mood? There might not be a specific reason you can think of, but just by listening to that song, you're suddenly uplifted. That song is an audible anchor as opposed to a physical one. On the flipside, do you have a particular song that for some reason you simply don't like? It may put you in a bad mood or make you feel low. You might even hate the song without knowing why. Again, that song is an audible anchor, only this time it's a negative anchor and not a positive one. So, now do you see how powerful an anchor might be?

You can even go as far as setting visual anchors. Imagine that you scratch your nose every time you give your wife a gift that makes her happy. She might not be aware of it, but her subconscious definitely will. So again, you can use this positive anchor when you need to. You can do this in reverse too and set a negative anchor. You may be asking why on earth would you want to set a negative anchor? Well, let's assume she wants to go to her mother's for the weekend. I'm sure I don't need to go too deep into the mother-in-law situation for you to get the idea why you might want to set a negative anchor if you don't really get on too well with the in-laws. It will give you a get-out-of-jail-free card if you use it for getting out of a family visit you don't want to do. There are plenty of other ways that NLP can be used and anchors can be set, but this should give you a reasonable introduction to NLP.

One last note on anchors before I get accused of being sexist. When I said you can use this technique to get your wife to go to your parents for the weekend, well ladies, you can also use it to get your husband to take out the trash or load the dishwasher!

You're welcome!

But there's so much more to NLP; as I said, it's a tree with many branches. It's an extremely powerful tool to have at your disposal and exceptionally useful. For many years my ex-partner had a fear of flying. After spending one morning of utilizing NLP techniques on her, before a flight from England to America, her fear of flying was pretty much gone, along with the pre-flight anxiety. There's certainly more to it, though, than just setting anchors. One of the most important areas is to build rapport with your subject first. Now I'm not going to go into a lengthy section of the process of building rapport, but it is extremely important to set a foundation using rapport in order to achieve your desired outcome (or their desired outcome, depending on the circumstances). I say this because it can be used to assist people in many areas, from ridding a person of depression to stopping a person from smoking and so much more. I have an ex-army friend, whom we'll call Sam Jones, who is now an NLP Master practitioner. After a long and outstanding career in the army and two tours of Iraq under his belt, he left the army and sadly suffered with PTSD (Post Traumatic Stress Disorder). I'm not going to go into all the details, but his PTSD is now gone through NLP, and he recently published his debut book.

Now you may be wondering why all this is relevant. Well as I mentioned, building rapport with your subject is highly important, and one of the lessons taught in Sam's NLP training courses is reading micro-expressions.

During Sam's training, the students are seated in a particular way and, for want of a better way to describe it, play a game. One person is told to think of somebody they really dislike, while the observer watches their facial expressions closely, paying particular attention to the Orbicularis Oculi (the muscle located in the eyelids – it is a sphincter muscle arranged in concentric bands around the upper and lower eye lids with its primary function being to close the eyes lids, which occurs when the muscle contracts). Then they are told to clear their thoughts for a moment before they think of somebody that they really like. Yet again, the observer watches the facial expressions closely. Given a moment to recompose themselves, they are then told to think of either one but not tell the observer. The observer has to determine which person they are thinking about (like or dislike) by reading their facial expressions and closely examining minute changes in the person's face which would normally be barely visible. This training game is a fantastic way to start off learning the basics of observing micro expressions. In time you can build up and look for rapid changes during conversation. A great way to do this is to talk casually with an associate and, at some point in the conversation, mention a person, food, or something else that you know they dislike. Watch closely for the shifts and movements in their facial expressions that can disappear as fast as they are formed. They will only be displayed for a fraction of a second, but with enough practice you'll find you can become really good at reading micro-expressions. I should point out here that there is a bit more to it than just playing the game, and a lot more training is given on reading micro-expressions first. With plenty of practice, though, you'll find it can become quite easy to gauge a person's true feelings or thoughts from the micro-expressions displayed on their face (even if it is only for less than a second).

If you still doubt the power of NLP, then maybe go to YouTube and watch some Derren Brown videos to see the real power of NLP at work!

Body Language Overview

In summary, the best way to give you a crash-course style lesson in body language is to explain that most of the time; any action where the body is exposed and vulnerable is a sign of openness and any defensive stance where the body is closely guarded (by anything from the arms to foreign objects) is a closed posture and shows high levels of discomfort. As I said, there is always an exception to every rule, and circumstances should always be taken into account. Always look at things in context with the situation, and it won't be long before you find yourself a master at reading body language.

Before we move on, I'm going to give you a few more things to look out for. If you don't already know, then figure out which is the dominant hand of the person you're in conversation with. If they are right-handed, then simply watch the right shoulder (and vice versa for left-handed) when you make a statement. If the persons shoulder moves back slightly (just a very slight and quick movement), then they disagree with the statement you have just made. It's easy to miss and takes a little practice, but it is one of the universals when it comes to body language. There aren't many of them, so this is a good area to practice with.

When a person is standing with their arms behind their back, look out for them gripping one arm with the opposite hand, as this is a sign of self-restraint. The higher the hand is up the arm, the more self-restraint they're practicing.

When a person is excited, they can become very animated as they talk. This is great because it allows you to learn so much about them.

Watch carefully as they talk and look out for which direction their hands go as they talk about something positive. If they move to the left, then that is the area associated with positivity. So when talking to them, if you want something to have a positive association attached to it, then you gesture to their left too. Notice I said their left! Make sure you don't miss that one. I imagine it's pretty obvious, but if their left has a positive association then it stands to reason their right has a negative association. So, if you're trying to convince the subject to go on a road trip, then gesture to their positive side as you talk about it. If you want to stay at home, then gesture to their negative side as you talk about it. It's very similar to the NLP techniques we talked about earlier in connection with setting anchors, only in this instance, the anchors are already set.

Look out for a bouncing leg or just general fidgeting when you're talking to a person. This is a surefire sign of excess energy usually caused by a dump of adrenalin that needs burning off. It could be through stress, it could be through nervousness, so as I keep saying, evaluate the situation and work out the cause from there.

I have hang-ups about teaching too much on the subject of body language in a book, not because I don't think it should be learned, but because when it's in a book, it's either in written form or pictures. My problem here is that people tend to then look for somebody holding a pose that matches the picture they've seen, instead of realizing that these actions might be made in a fleeting movement. Imagine, for example, somebody looking at the time on their wristwatch. They don't hold the position in front of them for a prolonged period of time. Instead, they take a glance at their watch, see the time and drop their hand to their side again. It's almost one smooth action and very brief. So remember, you're not looking at a painting here. In order to learn effectively you need to watch people. Whether it's live, while you're out and about, or on a screen, it's movements you're looking for rather than a held pose.

As I mentioned earlier, if you really want to get a great insight to the world of body language, search YouTube for *The Behaviour Panel*. That's a really great place to start and you can build your knowledge from there.

5. True Lies - The Truth Lies within the Statement

T his section is extremely important. Many people concentrate on the body language of a subject and end up looking past what is actually being said. I mentioned earlier each of these skills combined is what makes a person master deception detection to expert level. Mastering a single skill is great, but having an entire selection of skills to call upon and use in conjunction with each other can make you unrivalled.

This next particular area is a specialist subject, one I was lucky enough to receive training on by the actual creator. The SCAN (Scientific Content Analysis) technique was developed by Mr. Avinoam Sapir, a polygraph examiner, with a background in the Israeli Police Department in Jerusalem. Mr. Sapir holds bachelor's degrees in both Psychology and Criminology, and a master's in Criminology. He developed the SCAN technique by conducting extensive research into verbal communication, looking into the linguistic behavior used by people in communication. Although I had studied the analysis of statements previously and had become somewhat of a self-taught expert on the matter, I had the invite from a former Israeli intelligence friend to partake in Avinoam's course. I was one of the last students to be taken on by Avinoam before his retirement, so I consider myself extremely fortunate to have learned from the man himself. It's an area of extreme interest to me, and even with my self-educated experience that I had gained, I still learned so much from studying the SCAN technique. I was amazed. There were several revelations, and the time spent studying was well worth it. I have learned to analyze statements from other sources too. I have friends who are also experts in this area, and I have taken the time to learn from them as well as discuss our own methods, techniques, and thoughts on the subject.

This is going to be a pretty large section of the book because there's quite a lot to cover. I will give you some examples to work with; I will demonstrate what words and phrases can really mean when used in a sentence, and even more importantly, I will teach you how to detect the vital components missing from a sentence. If these components are absent, that's a huge red flag! Most people will overlook them, but you will now know exactly what to listen for.

I'm going to start things off very simple, and as you get to grips with the system, we can explore the more complex intricacies as we go. In most instances, I will give a case study or an example. At other times I will give an explanation of the reasons behind the lesson, but there will be some occasions where I will just give you a statement and its equivalent meaning without going too deep into the psychology or science behind it. This is for no other reason than that it's simply long-winded and boring. My aim here is to teach you as much as I can about the subject for practical application. If you really want to know more about the mechanics behind it, then I've no doubt there's a course or book that goes deeper into the subject specifics available out there somewhere. This book, however, is to help you learn how to master deception detection, not how it works or why.

With my qualifications in psychology, my extensive dealings with criminals, my training in the analysis of statements, and my background in investigations and intelligence gathering, I'm lucky enough to be able to see this subject from the forensic point of view, as well as the psychological point of view, with real world 'boots on the ground' experience too. Which for you as the reader is great because it means I can deliver my knowledge in this area for you to use to your advantage.

As I said, I'll start things off simple. Imagine that you have just handed someone a gift, they open it and say:

"It's lovely!"

You may think well there's nothing wrong with that. It's the kind of reaction you'd expect, right? Well, you might be surprised to find out that they don't like it. They don't want to offend you but they're not too keen on your gift.

How do I know? The lack of pronouns to start with. If they really like your gift they would say:

"I love it." as opposed to "It's lovely." You might be a little skeptical here, and I can understand why, but think about it like this, if you refer to yourself, you would use the pronoun "I", in the same way as if you were referring to someone else, where as you might use a pronoun like he, she, or they. It's the same if someone else were to refer to you. If, however, someone referred to you as an "it", all of a sudden you can see the context of how there's a difference between "I" vs. "it".

Compare:

Q: What do you think of Karen?

A: She's lovely.

To:

Q: What do you think of Karen?

A: It's lovely.

Doesn't sound quite so affectionate, does it?

You may still be a little skeptical but as you read on, more will be explained and everything will become clear. For the moment, just take on board that pronouns are extremely important. A pronoun demonstrates possession. A lack of them demonstrates distance. You will see how this is the case more and more, as we go further into analyzing statements.

There are certain words that when I explain the real meaning behind their use, it might seem counter-intuitive at first. For example, the sentence "I went shopping with my wife." would seem to most people to indicate that the man and his wife are close. In fact, quite the opposite is true. The word "with" actually denotes distance and not closeness.

Listen for someone saying, "I'm on the phone **with** my wife" as opposed to "I'm on the phone **to** my wife", the latter is preferable, and the former denotes distance in the relationship.

Going back to the previous sentence, "I went shopping **with** my wife" indicates that his wife went shopping and he just went along. If the sentence were structured something more like "My wife and I went shopping", this would be more indicative of closeness. The word "my" is a possessive, there's no use of the word "with", and as crazy at this seems, the distance between the two words "wife" and "I" are closer together than in the first sentence (maybe this is a subconscious and psychological occurrence). What I do know though, is people will place others in order of priority in the structure of their sentence. If ever you want to know your value to a person, listen to a how you are introduced among family members, if your name comes last, that tells you a lot. I'm sure you've heard the saying "last but not least", well sorry to have to tell you, but they're probably lying.

A great way to watch this unfold in real-time is to watch re-runs of the \TV program; Family Fortunes. The head of the household has to introduce themselves and tell the audience a little about their family. I love to hear a contestant say something along the lines of, "Hi, my name's Karen. I have 5 children, a horse, 2 dogs, a cat, a rabbit, 3 gerbils, and a husband called Brian."

Poor Brian probably doesn't know it, but he'd more than likely be better off alone. So, people are placed in the order of priority in a sentence, however, so are events. For example, "I went to town to get my nails done, do some clothes shopping, and get my hair done with my boyfriend." Did you notice how the boyfriend in the sentence was introduced last? That's because he is low on her priority list and nails, clothes, and hair are more important to her. If she had said "I went with my boyfriend to get my nails done, do some clothes shopping and have my hair styled", that would imply she valued her boyfriend higher than the other activities in the sentence.

To take it a step further, you can see how she started the sentence "I went with my boyfriend to…". This again indicates that she puts herself before her boyfriend. If the sentence had been "My boyfriend took me to get my nails done, go clothes shopping, and get my hair styled", this would indicate that she prioritizes her boyfriend above herself. So, listen to who comes first in a sentence and be aware of the distance of people within the sentence structure. Do they come first? Do they come second? Do other things come before them? Do they come last? What is the distance between the people in the sentence? Are they mentioned at the start of the sentence? In the middle? Or at the end?

Now that we've opened up one of the ways in which pronouns are important, let's look at some other ways they are relevant in a sentence. Below is a sentence for you to read and consider who is being talked about and how they are related to the speaker.

My sister is going to visit my parents this week, and I am going to see my mom and dad.

It seems like a relatively simple and clear statement, and ostensibly you would conclude that she is talking about her sibling, but let's look into it a little deeper.

It starts with "my sister" and says, is going to visit "my Parents", yet when she continues, she says: "and I am going to visit *my mom and dad*". *Parents* changed to *mom and dad*.

This is a highly valuable lesson in the analysis of statements, and one that should never be looked past: There are no synonyms in statement analyzing! (Much more on this later.)

I'll explain. Look once more at "*my* **sister** is going to visit *my* **parents**". If they were simply sisters, then wouldn't her parents be her sister's parents too? Wouldn't "*our* **parents**" be more fitting?

Before we go deeper into that, let's look at the next part of the sentence. "And I am going to see my mom and dad." The pronoun *my* denotes possession, they are *her* mom and dad but not her sister's, it appears. They might possibly be her sister's parents by means of adoption or she could possibly be a half-sister, if they were not, then the sentence would more likely read like this:

My sister and I are visiting our parents next week. Or I'm going with my sister to visit our mom and dad next week.

Either way, you can see the difference between this and the original sentence, which demonstrates the way information can be extrapolated from a simple sentence. We can dissect and examine the sentence to gain information from it's structure that's not said with the actual words, but by the way the words are being used. There will be more examples of this to follow.

It's now time to get serious. A study of a statement given in a rape case was the pivotal point of the entire case turning around, and the accuser confessing to a false allegation. The investigation completely changed direction by the use of a single pronoun. Just the use of the word 'we' on one occasion in her statement changed everything, and her story soon fell apart.

The girl's statement gave a detailed explanation of events leading up to the alleged crime. She used the pronouns 'I' when talking about herself and 'he' when talking about the man accused of raping her. She described the alleged incident in depth but then made a vital error. After the alleged rape she said: "After he zipped up his pants, **we** went back to the party."

At first this might not seem all that relevant, but I can assure you that it's of huge importance. There should never be use of the word 'we' after a rape has taken place. The word 'we' denotes closeness. It's a team word and highlights bond between two people. The victim of a rape would not use the pronoun we in a post-rape situation. Prior to a rape taking place, the use of the word 'we' is not significant as the two people might know each other, and the use of the word is justified, but after a rape, the victim should be using the words 'he' and 'I' in their description of events. I cannot express the importance of the word 'we' enough when it comes to analyzing statements. It really is a highly significant word that can change everything in the meaning of the statement.

Missing pronouns can be equally as significant as the pronouns used. For example, if someone were to talk about how their day started and said, "Got up, had breakfast. and went to work." then that tells us something that most people would not pick up on, he wasn't alone!

If he were to say, "I got up" as opposed to, "got up" then it shows he's talking about himself only, whereas the missing pronoun "I" indicates someone else was present when **they** "got up". If a person starts a statement without a pronoun, then somebody was with them.

The flipside to this is when I analyze resumes. I don't expect to find many pronouns, and if I come across the use of the pronoun 'I' too many times in a person's resume, then that raises concern and tells me more about the type of person they are than the actual words themselves.

I have helped companies avoid employing selfish, dishonest, and even dangerous prospective recruits on several occasions just by analyzing their resumes, some of which later proved to be possible near-misses, on account of events that unfolded. One person whose statement I analyzed in this way had been fired from a job for another company, and another was sent to prison. Your resume is technically your brochure of your working life. It's you selling yourself through your career experience, so it should be highlighting your best traits and choices, as well as the type of person you are. While I don't help people write their resume, I certainly know what to look for when examining one, and I can tell you that on many occasions I have come across resumes that have saved employers a lot of future problems. Staying on track, there's more to come on pronouns so let's look deeper into that now.

We're now going to look into the omission of pronouns when a person is talking. In the English language, a noun does not expose gender whereas a pronoun does, so with this in mind, take the following as a rule when it comes to conversation: If the person repeats the noun without using the pronoun their intention is to deliberately conceal the gender of the person they're talking about.

Example: "Yesterday I met my friend and my friend told me…"

This deliberately conceals the gender of the person they're talking about. If they didn't have intentions of concealing the gender, they would have said something more like:

"Yesterday I met my friend and **she** told me…"

So listen carefully to the use of nouns in place of pronouns in order to conceal gender, is that person saying he or she, and if not, then why?

A side note here is that while nouns do not expose gender in the English language (only pronouns do) Spanish, Italian, and Hebrew (and many other languages) expose gender in the nouns at the end of each word.

On another note, the repetition of pronouns indicates anxiety.

Because English is a unisex language, most gay people would refer to themselves as a 'person'.

Example: "I am a bit of a weird person." Or "Since I got divorced, I went in all different directions but recently I became a better person." Whereas, an alternative might be: "Since my divorce, I've tackled things alone, and I believe it's genuinely made me a better man." Or "Since my divorce, I've learned to cope alone, and it's certainly made me a better woman."

Of course this doesn't mean that heterosexuals don't ever refer to themselves as a person. Remember something being common does not make it exclusive.

I'd like to state that this is according to science based studies and not myself. This isn't opinion but based on global studies within this subject area. I only mention this to clarify that the information I've learned is not my own, so I'm not quoted later as saying something which could be conceived of being in any way offensive to anyone. I'm merely repeating what is currently considered factual, for the purpose of education and interest.

Continuing with this topic, homosexuality is referred to as an "Outside Issue" in polygraph terminology. Again, this is only mentioned for informational purposes which you might find interesting.

Pronouns continued

Over the last few years, I have examined many resumes that clients have asked me to look at in order to assist with making a decision as to whether a candidate is a suitable employee. On one occasion, I didn't need to read past the first paragraph to reach my decision. I was informed what the position entailed and the people the candidate would be working with, so I knew the person in this resume was not the right one for the job.

It started like this:

I'm looking for a job that will help me to advance in my career and help me to reach my full potential. I am highly experienced in many areas that could be of advantage to the right employer where I can exceed to over deliver on my allocated assignments. I work hard and I put the hours in, always going above and beyond what is expected of me. I have extensive experience in areas where I have had to improvise or work under my own initiative and I always excel, beating my targets and setting new records which I continually beat. I am always punctual, and I work harder than anyone I know. I look forward to being able to prove myself to the right employer.

At first you can be forgiven for thinking this is a reasonable sounding prospective candidate but let me ask you a question. How many times does the person use the pronouns; I, me, and my? Now count how many times they used the pronouns; you, us, and we.

The use of self-focused pronouns totals 22 times! Are any of them team-focused pronouns? None! That's right, not one. There's no mention about working as part of a team or getting on well with others or even being able to integrate in a department etc.

So, what does this tell us?

Does it indicate they're a bad person or self-centered? Does it show they believe it's "all about them"? The short answer is no. It could simply be that they're an independent and self-sufficient person. It could indicate they're used to working alone or a multitude of other possibilities. You would have to learn more about them to reach a truly educated decision. What it does tell us is that the person who wrote this resume is more than likely not suited to a position working in a team. There was no mention or evidence of teamwork, no team-focused pronouns, and no indication of the candidate being suited to the integration of themselves into a large department that works together. Compare this to the next sample below.

After more than 10 years of working in the XXXXXX department of XXXXXX our team has become more like a family to me than colleagues. We work well together to constantly further develop the needs and goals of our company, always giving more than is expected of us to help the smooth operations of the day-to-day success of our company and its employees.

Can you see the difference?

We could explore deeper to find out more about the two candidates but for the moment, we have established the difference that pronouns can make.

Let's go deeper into pronouns and criminal activity now.

Among the documents I examine, I frequently analyze insurance claims to look for potential fraud. On one occasion this was an example of how I established a fraudulent claim, initially based on the use of pronouns alone.

On the morning of the claim, I was on my way to the gym in my car. I had recently fitted a new massage seat pad in my car to make my drives in my car more enjoyable. I was no more than halfway to my destination when my car started making a noise I didn't recognize. I pulled into a rest area at the side of the road and the car shut off. The vehicle cut out and I couldn't figure out what was wrong with it. My cell phone was flat, so I had to leave the vehicle behind and walk to a gas station to dial for help. That was the last time I had seen the vehicle before I returned to find it on fire. I went back to the gas station to dial the fire department and waited for help.

There are two primary areas of concern here within the parameters of what we have discussed so far. As you can see, he starts off using the term 'my' and transitions to using the word 'the' in its place. Problem number two is the rule we set earlier on – There are no synonyms in Statement Analysis. The word 'car' turned into 'vehicle'. That was the second red flag after spotting the change from using pronouns to not using pronouns.

Let's break it down a little bit.

When the car was running fine on his drive to the gym it was 'his car', but when it broke down, he no longer considered it his. It was now referred to as 'the vehicle', indicating that in his mind, it had gone from being his possession (my car – The word 'my' is a possessive) to being an unwanted inanimate object. This denotes that the incident occurred at some point between the shift in syntax. In the claimant's mind, it was no longer his car. He'd already disowned it. The distancing language indicates this when he stops referring to it as his car (more on distancing language later).

Further examination of the claimant's statement revealed indications of guilt, and when interviewed, the claimant confessed that he had actually set fire to the vehicle himself.

As you can see in the two examples above, we have set the foundation for the use of pronouns and the rule of statement analysis – no synonyms. If the same thing is described using a different word, then something is wrong and should be looked at further.

On another note, a lack of pronouns should raise a red flag too (a 'red flag' or something that gets your attention enough to warrant further investigation, is called a Source Lead in interrogator parlance). If a statement is made with a lack of pronouns, then you should ask yourself why. An example of this would be a sentence something like the following:

Q: What did you do this morning?

A: Got up, had coffee, had some breakfast, and went to work.

You see how the answer had no pronouns in it at all and should have sounded more like this:

A: I got up, I had some coffee and breakfast, then I went to work.

We will cover the reasons for this a little later on as we explore analyzing statements in more depth, but for now, I thought it should be mentioned that a sentence with very few or no pronouns should cause you to pay attention and have you asking yourself why.

Now that we have established the fundamentals with regards to the use of pronouns and synonyms, we can further explore the science of analyzing statements. There is much more to it in every area of this topic, but at least you now have an understanding of how some of the moving parts work. To reiterate what have previously mentioned, sometimes I will give an explanation of how and why it works if I feel it's relevant and not too long-winded, at other times I will simply explain how you do it without a detailed explanation. You don't need to know every part of a combustion engine and how it works to drive the car. All you need to know is how to drive the car. The same applies here with analyzing statements. You don't always need to know how it's conducted in order to know how to use it. With that being said, I'll give a summarized explanation of the science behind it when it's necessary or I believe it's relevant. If you would like to know more and explore the subject deeper, then there are training courses available. For now, though, let's get into the next section, Statement Analysis and Crime.

In this next section I'm going to start with call transcripts to the emergency services. An investigation doesn't necessarily begin with the emergency services call by default, but it is where the contact from the person and the police starts, so this is where our lesson on analyzing what's being said will start. There will be some samples for us to look at and compare, in order to establish what is normally said by a genuinely concerned person in the event of an emergency, to a person showing signs of guilt and deception within their spoken words.

As I've stated already, this isn't necessarily where an investigation might begin, but for the person calling, this is their first contact with law enforcement, so a guilty person might feel the need to attempt to establish the foundation of their story. Let's examine the two following examples and see what the differences are.

Example 1

Operator: 911 What's your emergency?

Caller: I was out shopping, and I came home to find my husband dead on the floor, he fell on a knife and there's blood everywhere.

Now let's compare the first one to sample 2 and see what the differences are.

Example 2

Operator: 911 What's your emergency?

Caller: Help, please send help. My husband is bleeding! There's a knife and I don't know what to do. Please can you send someone to help him?

Which one do you think shows signs of guilt, and which one do you believe is genuinely trying to get help for the victim? These are of course over-exaggerated examples of a 911 call, but I have come across some that are extremely similar to these in real life scenarios.

We will now explore them as if they are real transcripts and highlight the areas that demonstrate possible guilt.

Starting with example 1, she begins the call with "I was out shopping". Remember earlier when we established that people will prioritize what is most important to them in the structure of the sentence, like poor Brian coming last to all of his wife's pets? Well, the same applies here. The caller prioritizes the need to establish where she was. It's her main priority to have it on record that she was out shopping. She then continues to say, "I came home", again further reinforcing the fact she was not there at the time of the crime. She continues with "... to find my husband dead on the floor." Now he may not be dead, or he might still be able to be saved with medical attention. We don't know this and it's possible that she doesn't either. There are too many variables that could be argued here, so we will move onto the next part where she then states, "he fell on a knife." Well, how does she know he fell on a knife? She's already established that she wasn't there. Somebody could have broken in and stabbed him and could still be in the house. He could have stabbed himself. There are multiple possibilities. There's no way at this point that it can be determined with 100% accuracy that he "fell on a knife". What this suggests is, yet again, she's trying to create a story and lead people to take a particular path with their thoughts that she is pointing them to.

Compare the first example to the second example where the caller's first words are, "Help, please send help." As you can see, her priority in this example is getting help. She then states, "My husband is bleeding", not that he's dead! "There's a knife", not that he fell on a knife. Again, she doesn't know what happened because she wasn't there, all she knows is that there's a knife. She tells the operator that she doesn't know what to do and again begs for help. This is more like a caller whose priority is getting help and not establishing the foundation for an alibi.

Of course, not all 911 calls are this easy to compare and spot the signs of guilt (if it was that easy anybody could do my job), but the basics are there for you to learn. Like we previously covered, get good at the basics and then move on to the more advanced material later. That is the best way to master the skills.

I'll give you another two samples and see if you can work out which one is the guilty party and which one is a genuine request for help.

Example 1

Operator: 911 What's your emergency?

Caller: I need an ambulance for my wife. She's had an accident and she's bleeding. I don't know what happened. Can you send help?

Example 2

Operator: 911 What's your emergency?

Caller: My Wife needs help, she's bleeding. Please hurry.

We'll start with example 1. This one might be a little more difficult for some but again look at who he prioritizes. He starts the sentence with "I". He says "I need..."; he then goes on to say she's had an accident. Does he know this for sure? Was he there? Judging by his next sentence, what would you say? He makes a vital error here and adds what I call an "unnecessary negative". He says, "I don't know what happened." Well, this is what the operator would naturally assume, and if they didn't, they would ask. The fact that he volunteered it without being asked raises a red flag.

Imagine a scenario where I'm intruding myself on a TV show, or at a party, and the reaction I would get if I said: "Hi I'm Gavin Stone. I don't steal money from the petty cash at work, and I'm from England. Pleased to meet you."

Can you see how crazy it sounds? That's an Unnecessary Negative. It's not required. Nobody would be thinking that I steal from the petty cash from work, so why would I say that? The only reason somebody I just met would be thinking that, is if I'd said it.

When it's put like this, you can see how insane an Unnecessary Negative is, yet they are frequently overlooked. From now on, pay close attention and they should become a little more obvious to you.

Another example is if someone said, "Hey somebody broke the window on your car. I don't know if they threw a brick through it, but it's smashed."

It would be apparent they knew that somebody threw a brick through it, or they wouldn't have said that. If they saw a brick on the seat of your car, they would say something more like, "It looks like someone threw a brick through it." Or "There's a brick on the seat, it looks like somebody threw it at your window." If they didn't know how it happened, they would simply say "Hey, your car window's been smashed", or "hey, the window's been smashed on your car." There would be no need for someone to add, "I don't know how it happened." at the end.

Of course, if they did know how it happened because they saw someone do it then they would say that also. Again, no need for the Unnecessary Negative.

Finally, with the caller in example 1 he lastly says, "Can you send help?". Once more this is showing his priorities. The last thing he wants is the ambulance for his wife. He wants to establish his innocence first.

With example 2, he opens his sentence with, "My wife needs help"; his wife and getting her help are his priorities. He states that she's bleeding. There's no Unnecessary Negative, nothing stated about how it happened or anything else, he simply wants help for his wife and finishes with "please hurry".

Once more, there's a lot more to it than this, but my aim here is to get you to grips with the fundamentals of analyzing statements and how it works. There are so many more areas when it comes to the scientific analysis of statements, and teaching that would be an entire book by itself. This book is about deception detection, so we have covered some of the areas you need to know when it comes to finding a lie when analyzing a person's statement. Before we end this section, I'm going to finish it by asking you to be more aware of a person's reply. This alone can be a huge indication of deception. After their reply, you simply ask yourself, did they answer the question? I'll give you an example.

The standard issue pen at MI6 is a Pentell Rollerball. There's a story behind how it came about which dates back to the cold war. MI6 officers would send messages back to HQ using invisible ink. A particular method was used to retrieve the hidden messages when they were back in England, making the ink reappear and be readable again. As an extra layer of security, the officer would write a letter with a standard pen in the normal format with nothing of any relevance at all, then seal it inside the envelope. The address was then written on the front of the envelope, and the secret message on the reverse side of the envelope. It was a simple decoy that meant if the Russians intercepted the letter, they would open and discard the envelope and waste their time trying to find hidden codes or messages within the contents of the letter, while overlookeding the secret message that was on the reverse of the envelope. Sometimes, the simplest way of hiding things can be the most effective. But before I digress, let's get back to the reason I bring this to your attention. On a fateful day in the MI6 headquarters, a letter from Moscow arrived and when the method of revealing the hidden message was implemented, two sets of writing appeared instead of one. The one was the actual secret message, the other was an address written in mirror image in a completely different style of handwriting.

This was a momentous discovery. It would seem there was a pen out there, available to the general public, that had the ability to send hidden messages with a sort of disappearing ink. MI6 concluded that the envelope they had received had been pressed up against another one during its travels, and the ink from the second envelope had left an invisible impression on the one they had received, becoming visible again when they went through the process they normally used to make the disappearing ink visible.

This had benefits that were twofold. The first was the fact they could now use this new mystery pen to see what they were writing before it was sent home, as opposed to the previous method that was invisible when writing and which nobody could see until the method of revealing it was executed. The second was that, whatever pen this was that was out there, it was available to the general public, entailing deniability. They couldn't be questioned for having a weird pen that wrote invisible messages, it was just an everyday ordinary pen to the rest of the world. To add to that, the new system of writing the message and then pressing it against the outside of the envelope provided a second layer of deniability. If the letter was intercepted and the message was discovered, being on the outside of the envelope meant that it could have happened at any time and been put there by anyone, meaning any evidence it provided was at best circumstantial. The only weak link would have been the original letter that was written before being pressed onto the envelope, which any respectable intelligence officer would have burned immediately.

There was great excitement over this new information, and MI6 went on a mission to discover exactly which pen had this amazing feature. A huge budget and lot of time and resources was put into buying every single make, type, and model of pen available to the public, and then each one was tested. A message was written on a blank piece of paper, pressed against another piece of paper, then had to undergo the process used to reveal to see if the ink would appear or not. Thousands of pens and many exhausting hours of testing eventually lead to the elusive pen being the Pentell Rollerball. From that day, it was bulk bought and became the standard issue pen to all MI6 intelligence officers.

I had two of these particular pens and carried one or the other around with me for many years, regularly replacing the cartridge because I used them that much (never for writing anything sensitive though!). These days the officers at MI6 don't have any sort of standard issue stationery per se, the theory is quite simple; if something works, use it. Especially if it's openly available and even more so if it's available to the public in the country you're operating in. Most of the time, intelligence officers must work with whatever they can get their hands on, so this usually means everyday off the shelf stuff that can be bought by anyone. Imagine how awkward it would be landing in a foreign country trying to explain to customs the reason you have a suitcase loaded with devices that can listen through walls, X-ray camera equipment, or a lock-pick set inside a dodgy credit card. Instead, you're taught how to make lock picks etc. out of everyday items. Of course, your kit has to match your cover story; it would be no good posing as a printer earning an average wage, sporting a 1000k Jaeger Couture watch, but that's a whole different topic for another book. Publicly available doesn't always mean plausible. My Pentell Rollerball on the other hand is affordable to pretty much anyone.

Forgive me seemingly digressing but I wanted you to know the relevance of my pen and how it comes into play in the following example. On one occasion, I was working at an army barracks in the

UK when I realized I'd lost my pen. I'd put it down somewhere and forgotten to pick it up. Upon retracing my steps, I remembered that I'd left it in the Ops room a couple of days ago. (In civilian terms, that's a large room where the intricate details of a military operation are planned. In military terms, it's where we drink coffee and chat shit.) I went back to the Ops room and couldn't find it. I asked around and established that the last person to be in the Ops rooms was Fred (not his real name) before locking it up and nobody had signed the keys out since. It was no big issue, he was due to start a shift later that day, so I decided to ask him if he'd picked up my pen.

I asked him when he came in and he replied,

"I wasn't in yesterday." And carried on walking past me to the locker room.

At first, I accepted his answer and was about to dismiss the whole thing, when I realized something; he hadn't answered my question. He'd given me a response.

It took me a moment, but it dawned on me that his response sounded like an answer and in fact, it was an answer, but not to the question I had asked. If I hadn't paid close attention, I would have accepted his response and moved on. In this instance, I pursued the line of questioning tactfully and recovered my pen from Fred who, when given an out, realized that he had picked it up, apparently by mistake.

So with this in mind, I had learned a very valuable lesson, one that I am going to pass on to you. Pay very close attention to the response a person gives you when you ask them a question, then ask yourself;

did they answer the question I asked them, or did they respond with something to pacify me, knowing I would accept what they'd said and drop the question.

This particular area of statement analysis is probably one of the most prominent when it comes to deception detection. So I'll finish this section here by saying that the method of analyzing the reply you receive combined with reading body language and other methods you're going to learn in this book are extremely powerful tools to have at your disposal, so as with any other methods I have written about, practice them in your everyday world. Ask people you know a few awkward questions and listen to how they respond, and if they actually answer the question or if they evade it.

It should go without saying it would be best to use a little common sense here; the last thing I want is to hear that some poor fellow got sacked for asking his boss if he's having an affair behind his wife's back or some other crazy story involving awkward questions. So please put a little thought into what and whom you are asking, and the possible ramifications, before you start interrogating the CEO of the company you work for in an elevator ride!

Bonus material

Three is number of choice for liars. This little section is just an added extra that you might find useful. It appears that liars have a favorite number, which is number three. I'm sure you have had experiences in the past where you've heard things like: "Three times I came around and there was no sign of you!" Or "Three grand was stolen from my drawer." Even, "Three times I tried and it still wouldn't work". Now, that's not to say for definite that someone is lying when they say the number three. It is, however, the number that liars default to most of the time when questioned. The reason I suspect is because it seems a believable number, it's not over the top and is still more than once when trying to stress a point. As I said, it's not a definitive sign of a lie but it should be taken into consideration when questioning someone. If they have to make a number up on the spot when they're lying, percentage wise, it's a higher chance they will pick the number three if they're attempting to deceive you. So listen out for the number three. It may be the truth they're telling but with the material you will learn from the rest of this book, you'll be able to combine it with your other knowledge and have a better chance of spotting if they're lying to you.

6. Eye Accessing Cues, Eye Contact & Blink Rate

This next area is one of my personal favorites and my go-to method if I want to reveal deception. This skill can be used alone but like before is strengthened with the added skill from other areas. It's not only one that I love but is also a favorite of a friend of mine Lena Sisco.

Lena Sisco is a former Naval Intelligence Officer and Marine Corps certified interrogator who served in the Global War on Terror conducting hundreds of interrogations. She is a published author, keynote speaker, former TEDx speaker, and an expert witness on a court TV show. She is a keynote speaker for the International Spy Museum and featured in the Mata Hari exhibit.

Since 2003, Lena has been training the Department of Defense, government agencies, law enforcement, and private sector industries in interviewing and interrogation, statement analysis, body language, detecting deception, elicitation, and change leadership.

Lena is also certified in Organizational Change Management and received her certificate in the Psychology of Leadership from Cornell University. She has a master's from Brown University in Archaeology, and her BA is in Anthropology.

In 2013, Lena started her own company, called The Congruency Group, of which I am also a consultant and trainer. So when I say she's an authority in the industry, I really mean it. With the above being a short summary of her career, you can take it from me that she is more than a master in deception detection. Her experience in Guantanamo Bay military prison makes her a prime example of one of the world's experts in this area. We co-host a Clubhouse room on Thursdays where we share lessons on interrogation, elicitation, lie detection, and so much more. We've discussed Eye Accessing Cues many times and both agree it's a highly valuable area to have at our disposal. Now we can pass this skill on to you.

This next part (for which I am extremely grateful) is by Lena herself and I will continue with a little more on Eye Accessing cues, Eye Contact and Blink Rate at the end.

Lena:

Eye Movements CAN Tell You if Someone is Lying; If You Baseline

There is a lot of controversy over the Neuro-Linguistic Programming (NLP) eye accessing cues model, or eye pattern movement analysis tool, and its use in detecting deception. Scientists, psychologists, and NLP certified trainers refute the idea that NLP can be used to monitor eye movements to detect deception. The NLP eye pattern movement theory regarding lie-spotting is said to be poorly supported scientifically, and that the tests contained errors and were thus discredited by the scientific community. I have conducted hundreds of interrogations and interviews and thousands of training hours where I tested this theory, and I will tell you that if you used correctly, eye movement patterns can tell you if someone is lying or not.

In 1976, John Grinder and Richard Bandler developed the theory of NLP for the purpose of making explicit models of human excellence. They explored the relationship between eye movements and the different senses, as well as the different cognitive processes associated with the brain hemispheres. They hypothesized that people tap into their cognitive processes while communicating through different means: auditory, visual, and kinesthetics. Bandler and Grinder claimed that NLP can treat problems such as eating & learning disorders, curing phobias, co-dependency issues, physical ailments, unwanted habits and behaviors, to name but a few. NLP is also used to achieve personal successes such as leadership and health and overall well-being. As an interrogator, I used NLP as a completely different tool; I used it to detect deception.

Bandler and Grinder created an Eye Accessing Model where you could identify if a person was retrieving true memories or creating them based on where their eyes shifted.

Eye Movements and NLP

by Robert Dilts[2]

The notion that eye movements might be related to internal representations was first suggested by American psychologist William James in his book Principles of Psychology (1890, pp. 193-195). Observing that some forms of micromovement always accompany thought, James wrote:

---

[2] http://www.nlpu.com/Articles/artic14.htm

"In attending to either an idea or a sensation belonging to a particular sense-sphere, the movement is the adjustment of the sense-organ, felt as it occurs. I cannot think in visual terms, for example, without feeling a fluctuating play of pressures, convergences, divergences, and accommodations in my eyeballs...When I try to remember or reflect, the movements in question. . .feel like a sort of withdrawal from the outer world. As far as I can detect, these feelings are due to a literal rolling outwards and upwards of the eyeballs."

What James is describing is well-known in NLP as a visual eye-accessing cue [eyes moving up and to the left or right for visualization]. James' observation lay dormant, however, until the early 1970's when psychologists such as Kinsbourne (1972), Kocel et al. (1972) and Galin & Ornstein (1974) began to equate lateral eye movements to processes related to the different hemispheres of the brain. They observed that right-handed people tended to shift their heads and eyes to the right during "left hemisphere" (logical and verbally oriented) tasks, and to move their heads and eyes to the left during "right hemisphere" (artistic and spatially oriented) tasks. That is, people tended to look in the opposite direction of the part of the brain they were using to complete a cognitive task.

"As a result of these studies, and many hours of observations of people from different cultures and racial backgrounds from all over the world, the following eye movement patterns were identified." (Dilts, 1976, 1977; Grinder, DeLozier and Bandler, 1977; Bandler and Grinder, 1979; Dilts, Grinder, Bandler and DeLozier, 1980):

- Eyes Up and Left: Non-dominant hemisphere visualization - i.e., remembered imagery (Vr).

- Eyes Up and Right: Dominant hemisphere visualization - i.e., constructed imagery and visual fantasy (Vc).

- Eyes Lateral Left: Non-dominant hemisphere auditory processing - i.e., remembered sounds, words, and "tape loops" (Ar) and tonal discrimination.

- Eyes Lateral Right: Dominant hemisphere auditory processing - i.e., constructed sounds and words (Ac).

- Eyes Down and Left: Internal dialogue, or inner self-talk (Ad).

- Eyes Down and Right: Feelings, both tactile and visceral (K).

- Eyes Straight Ahead, but Defocused or Dilated: Quick access of almost any sensory information; but usually visual."

Here's the catch; this model does not apply to every individual. I have encountered numerous people whose eyes go everywhere but up and to the right when they lie. I have also met people whose eye movements follow this chart and anchor up and to the right when they are recalling a rehearsed lie or making one up on the spot. How is that possible?

We use two types of memories when we are being questioned about an event. If we are telling the truth and the event happened, we have to recall the details from our episodic memory – our autobiographical memory. If we decide to suppress the truth and create a lie, or recall a lie we have already created, we access our semantic memory, which is our memory of known information. For example, you may not have ever been to Alaska, but I bet you know something about Alaska. Since we cannot create a lie out of nothing, we create it from known bits of information in our semantic memory that we link together to form a fictitious event – which is why our lies usually lack detail. Either way, if a person decides to tell the truth or lie, they have to access their memory, episodic or semantic respectively.

I will explain the myth behind NLP and why scientists refute it, but how you can still use it as detecting deception tool. The myth is eye movements alone can tell if a person is lying or telling the truth; this is simply not true. Just as in reading body language, you need to baseline a person's verbal and nonverbal behaviors when they are most relaxed and look for clusters of behavioral indicators, both deceptive and truthful. The eyes alone can't tell you if a person is being deceptive. Also, no indicator is 100% accurate, not even NLP eye pattern movements. To use eye pattern movements as a tool for detecting deception, you have to do two things: first you have to baseline a person's eye pattern movements, and second, since peoples' eyes move around a lot when they speak, you have to monitor where they tend to anchor the most.

Eye movements happen when we access cues; they can tell us when ideas, images and thoughts are being constructed or remembered or a combination of both. They can also tell us if others feel sorrow or remember sounds, but it changes from person to person; eye pattern movements are not the same with everyone, nor should they be read that way. When using NLP, know that it is critical to first baseline a person's normal eye patterns, because they may be completely opposite to what that chart states. Once you get a baseline, now look for changes in the patterns; they looked up and to the left when recalling their last job, but they now are looking up and to the right to recall their last address. If both sets of information require recall, and not construction, the eyes should be going to same area both times, not different ones.

Here's a secret: if you want to baseline someone within seconds, ask them this question and see if their eyes go up to the right or to the left, "what is the fifth word in the Pledge of Allegiance, or the Star-Spangled Banner, or the prayer Hail Mary, etc.". Use whatever makes more sense for your target. My mother is very religious so I would ask her about Hail Mary, whereas I would ask a stranger wearing a football jersey about the Star-Spangled Banner. Almost immediately, your target's eyes will either go up to right or left; according to the chart they should go to the left, and in most cases I find that to be true, but there are some variations. For instance, if you ask about the Star-Spangled Banner, it is a song, so your target may be recalling an auditory sound, not a vision of the words themselves, so they may look to the left at eye level and not up to the left.

I frequently hear NLP and body language being referred to as "voodoo" sciences because people believe these theories are a bit mystical, kind of like seeing ghosts. There are some people who believe in ghosts or spirits because of personal experiences, and some who think these people are not of sound mind. Who's to say whether or not ghosts exist? Who's to say NLP eye pattern movements can detect deception? Those who have experienced it.

Over the past two decades I have been baselining my litigants', detainees', and suspects' eye pattern movements, and I will tell you that I have observed that when people lie, their eye gaze deviates from their baseline eye movement behavior. Now, I don't use this cue alone to determine if a person is lying. That would have been foolish. I look for clusters of other verbal and nonverbal deceptive indicators to ensure I am seeing deceptive behaviors.

Let's dissect the word itself: Neuro-Linguistic Programming. You can see that there are three distinct components that, combined together, create this theory, or tool, that can be used to solve problems, whether it's helping detect lies or curing a snake phobia. They are: neurology, language and programming. Neurology is how our brains function; it's how we think. Language is how we communicate. Programming manages our patterns of thoughts and our mental and emotional behaviors.[3]

As we humans develop emotionally, socially, and cognitively, our life experiences register in our minds and are recalled by their association with a sense: visual (sight), auditory (hearing), kinesthetic (emotional but includes touch), olfactory (smell), and gustatory (taste). These senses are referred to as "modalities" in NLP. "Submodalities" further define the modality. For example, when I smell the specific scent of a Yankee Candle ("sunset", to be precise), I am instantly taken back to the late 1980's when my best friend Tina and I would spend endless carefree summer days at the beaches in RI. When I hear the faint sound of church bells off in the distance, I am reminded

----

[3] http://www.steverrobbins.com/nlpschedule/random/police-interrogation.html#footnote2

of the spring-time in the house I grew up in located two blocks from a church. Submodalities are the details associated with the 5 senses that are anchored to a memory or experience. Therefore, it makes sense that the NLP model is based on assessing cues (recalling), or constructing cues (creating), although each can happen when assessing and constructing information because people may not be assessing or constructing the information you think they are based on your questions.

Eye movement is a normal activity when we are talking to someone. We do not stare people down, it's rude, even in the United States. If you are doing business with an American, you'd better make sure you have a firm handshake and direct eye contact. Sometimes we tend to push both of those things a little too far as we crush an individual's hand and stare them down. In other cultures, it is rude to make direct eye contact. I found this out when I was in Korea. Even in our efforts to look people in the eyes when we talk to them, our eyes will still wander about. The NLP theory is that they wander to certain spots or areas, though, for a reason.

When we assess or construct cues, we may think of a time when we felt sorrow, or it may make us engage in an internal dialogue. Going back to the example of when I smell the Sunset Yankee Candle, I instantly have an emotional response (kinesthetic) of feeling happy and carefree, so if I am describing those days to someone my eyes may go down and to the right as I have this kinesthetic experience when recalling those memories. We may have a strong emotional response first before we go to logic and reason to answer the question and tell a story or vice versa. This is why to simply state if a person's eyes go up to the right they are lying and constructing information is not a sound conclusion. Even when people lie, they will tend to access some truth. For example, if a teenager wanted to lie about why they came home past curfew last night, and they say it was because their friend's car broke down, the car may really exist as an image in their mind so they will recall the image of the car and their eyes will go up to the left (visual recall), but they may have an sense of emotional guilt and sadness because they are lying so their eyes may go down to the right (kinesthetic, emotional feelings), and then they may remember truly being in a car the last time it broke down hearing their parents yelling at the car and their eyes may go straight and left (auditory recall). Never once during this lie did the teenager's eyes go up and to the right (visual construct) which would tell us they are constructing the information, hence making it up. So how on earth can we use, how I used, NLP as a tool in detecting deception with all those caveats? I will explain how I use it still today in the following paragraphs.

NLP is still linking up neurology, how we think, with language, what we say, and programming, our emotional state at the time we are thinking and speaking.

Gavin:

As you can see, Lena and I are both serious advocates of Eyes Accessing Cues and so is another person I happen to hold in very high esteem, whom I mentioned earlier, and that's Greg Hartley. So, despite what you may have previously heard, it is a go-to technique of some of the world leaders in deception detection. I have used it many times successfully and will continue to.

As a qualified practitioner in NLP, I can tell you how useful it has been, but the most important thing to remember is this: the chart (used above by Lena) is not set in stone. It is a template for what is known in the NLP world as an NOP or Normally Organized Person. In some places, it is said that the chart is simply reversed for left-handed people. This isn't the case either. The chart is subjective. It changes for each person. The N.O.P. is not a one-size-fits-all! It is set in a way that is frequently the most common for a lot of people, and some areas are constant, but you have to adapt it for each person you meet.

So instead of looking at the chart and trying to align it to a person you're talking to, talk to the person and see where their eyes go to as they recall memories or think about things they've heard or felt, and make your own chart for that individual. You will have to do this for every person you meet, but once you have established where their eyes go for each subject you know their baseline and it will always remain the same.

Eye contact

Here is an area that might surprise many people due to the common misconception that liars cannot maintain eye contact when lying. In fact, quite the opposite is true. For the duration of the statement when a person is lying, they will maintain eye contact. This is purely because they want to watch carefully to see your reaction and don't want to miss a thing. They will more than likely not even blink, allowing them to take in as much information as possible. When you finally react, this is the point at which they might blink or even give a flutter of rapid blinks, if the stress level is heightened. All of this depends upon the situation and your reaction to them, of course. As I have said before, dynamic assessment is key.

I have had situations in the past whereupon quizzing an individual, after he answered, the prolonged eye contact was what made me doubt his response. He looked straight at me and didn't follow up, keeping his eyes locked on mine the entire time. That alone was enough to prompt me to pursue my questioning only to find out later that I was correct to do so, and the individual was lying. Had he not locked his wide-open baby blues on mine throughout his entire reply and kept them there afterwards, I might not have pushed much further, because up until that point, I had no reason to disbelieve him. That singular action was all it took to make me want to probe further and then get to the truth.

While we're on the subject of eyes, I'm going to talk about another action the eyes can make that can indicate someone is not being truthful. It's what I call eyeball-pinball. Referring to the action made by the eyes as you ask them a question. You see their eyes dance around making the motion of a pinball bouncing around inside a pinball machine, rapid and jerky tiny eye movements. In the world of psychology, the official terminology for this action is a Trans-derivational search (often abbreviated to TDS), meaning when a search is being conducted for a fuzzy match across a broad field.

The reason for this is the brain is searching through a selection of answers and as it accesses different thoughts and memories from different areas of the brain, the eyes make this rapid movement of flashing around to different positions in sequence of your thoughts. Have you ever heard the saying "my life flashed in front of my eyes" when a person has had a near death experience? Well, the reason for that is because their brain panicked. In the seconds before imminent death, your brain freaks out for a moment and rapidly scans through your entire life's memories to search for something to use from previous similar experiences, in order to stay alive. It's looking for a tool from all of your collected memories to help preserve you. If it hasn't been in this near-death situation before, it's got nothing to compare to in order to see what it has used previously to keep you alive, so it quickly scans every memory you've ever made to find the closest scenario and see if there's anything there that can be of use in this situation you are in now. For most people, it comes up with nothing, that's why they simply freeze and squint. The lucky ones that live to tell the story of their near-death experience, tell you how their life flashed before their eyes, and now you know why.

This is a very similar reaction to when you catch a person off-guard with a question they weren't expecting. Their eyes dance around as they panic, and the mind scrambles to come up with an answer that they know has worked previously in similar circumstances and could work this time too.

With this in mind, some people process information extremely rapidly and might be thinking about the path of several answers simultaneously. It may be because they are being deceitful and trying to decide the best way to steer the conversation. It might also be that they are confused by the question and are trying to make sense of what you asked. This time, their mind is searching through memories to compare similar questions or experiences from their past to decide how to answer appropriately. Once more, look for a cluster of other tells, like signs of discomfort, a change in their demeanor or speech rate, tone, and pitch. Some of these we will cover later, but these clusters will help to identify if a person is feeling uncomfortable or stressed by your question as opposed to confused.

I also feel it's important to express once more that you have to be aware of the person's baseline before you jump to any conclusions with these techniques. There are people out there that are suffering with anxiety and struggle to hold eye contact for long or at all. There are also people who naturally keep eye contact for longer than others. The situation needs to be taken into account as well as the person. Lovers having a romantic meal together are more likely to maintain eye contact with each other as they talk too. When a woman is sexually attracted to a man, she will stare at him for longer as he and she talk. This is a biological factor. Her eye contact is to take in as much as possible about her potential mate. Her pupils will dilate, and her blink rate will decrease. The reason for this is because she wants to learn as much as she can about him before she decides to go any further. The result is wide eyes and less blinking to send as much information to the brain as possible.

Blink Rate

Lastly in this section we're going to talk about blink rate. This is an area of great value to indicate a person's stress rate. The average person's blink rate is approximately 12 per minute. This can go up to as much as 100 in times of stress and as low as four or five when a person is either relaxed or concentrating on something, like watching a film they're really into for example.

Of course, you don't have to stare like a psycho at them counting their blinks for long periods of time to work out an average. Simply count how many times they blink over the course of six seconds and multiply it by 10 to get the answer.

As I've said before, the higher the blink rate the higher the stress levels but don't attempt to quantify it for a "one size fits all" purpose. As I continually stress, and will continue to reiterate throughout this book, you must treat each person on an individual basis. Instead of looking for a particular number of blinks to determine if a person is stressed or not, you should be looking for change.

Some people blink a lot, others have a lower blink rate naturally. So all of this needs to be taken into consideration before you try and work out if they're stressed or relaxed. Start by getting their blink rate in a standard situation. Only then will you know if it has increased, decreased or remains the same when they're in the process of being questioned on a particular subject. Once again, you are not looking for a specific number, you're looking for change.

As well as blink rate which refers to the amount of time a person blinks within a period of time, another area to pay attention to is the blink speed. This is the amount of time it takes a person to complete the motion of the eyelid closing and fully reopening again. Most of the time it is relatively quick however, in some instances the eyelid can close and remain closed for longer than normal before slowly opening again. This slowed blink speed can be a form of "Eye Blocking".

There are several ways a person can perform the act of eye blocking. Like the example above, a slow blink is one but sometimes you can see a person covering their eyes with the tips of their thumb and forefinger (this is not a definitive sign of a lie but rather a signal of stress). Remember to assess the situation here. It might be you causing the stress as opposed to the question or questions. For the moment, though, we're going to concentrate on a standard scenario where you're asking a person a question they are uncomfortable with. They may make the above action of rubbing their eyes with their thumb and fingertips (I've seen people remove their glasses just to make this action). Another form of eye blocking is when a person holds their hand flat out above their eyes, like they're trying to shield themselves from a bright light. Their thumb usually running down the side of their head pointing backwards and their hand acting like a peak of a ball cap. They'll usually be looking down when this happens.

Imagine being at a board meeting and one of your colleagues starts to tell an embarrassing story to the boss. You know what's coming so you look down at the table, put your hand to your forehead and maybe even start rubbing your eyebrow a little as he talks. You might put your elbow on the table and you do all you can to avoid eye contact, simply because you're aware of what's about to be said. This is a form of eye blocking. The sheer embarrassment forces you to look away. This level of uncomfortable conversation is a perfect example of how and when this action might be seen. So make a mental note of it. Look out for it when communicating with other people.

The reason we block our eyes is quite simple. Just like when we were children, we used to hide under the covers at the sight of something we didn't like, the same applies to adults when we don't want to visualize the ugliness of the situation, or the lie being told. It's a way of psychologically 'not being there'. Of course, we can't start pulling covers over our head, so we do the only alternative available to us, we close or cover our eyes. Even if it's momentarily, it helps us cope with the situation mentally.

Before we end this section, I would also like to point out that as before; every situation needs to be handled with an open-minded approach. It will not only change for each individual; it will also change depending upon whom that individual is talking to. On average we maintain eye contact for around 7 seconds when in conversation with someone we like, that drops to around 4 or 5 seconds when talking to someone we dislike. Yet another factor to take into account when monitoring the eyes is pupil dilation. A person's pupils will dilate when they see someone they find attractive, become scared, or if the light around them lowers. On the flipside, they will constrict if the light levels are higher, or if they see something they dislike. In relation to this, a person's pupils with also constrict as a form of eye blocking too. So if they are in an uncomfortable situation, becoming stressed or being deceptive, their pupils may constrict. It's easier to see with light colored eyes than dark but it can be spotted if you look carefully.

To finish this section on the eyes and eye movement, I will wrap up with one last nugget of information. When I mentioned earlier about liars looking away when they speak being less likely, when they do look away, pay attention to the direction their eyeballs go as they do. In short, vertical is good and horizontal is bad, most of the time. People's eyes move down as they talk in a submissive fashion, or they can go upwards in an attempt to retrieve a memory, even up and down to each corner. But just left or right, that should be noted as a possible issue. As I say so many times, get their baseline first. When training law enforcement officers, I tell them to watch a suspect's eyes closely upon the approach and as they talk. If their eyes and head move sideways together, they're looking for an escape route ad preparing to make a run for it!

This same information I'm going to give to you but for use in a different context. If a person's eyes are moving sideways simultaneously with their head, they might not actually be preparing to physically run but that is their preferred intention, escape. They want to escape the questioning and get out of there. Once again, it doesn't mean they're lying, it simply means they don't like what's going on, or what's being talked about and so on. It's down to you to decide if it's the questioning or the circumstances that are making the subject perform these actions.

All of this is something you have to learn whilst watching other people of course, whether live or on TV or YouTube, because quite simply, you can't see your own eyes move in the mirror for starters. You can, however, try to be more aware of which location your own eyes go to in certain circumstances, but this will only give you a baseline for yourself.

7. Beliefs & Biases

Biases and belief play a huge role in impairing someone's ability to detect lies. I'm sure you've heard the saying "love is blind". Going back a few years, I had a friend called Mark. Now Mark was a great guy but the love of his life, Maria, was an extremely popular individual. Now it would probably be wrong of me to imply that she was promiscuous, but she used to choose underwear by judging how warm it would keep her ankles. Mark would constantly suspect Maria was doing things she shouldn't, but every time he asked her, she would give an explanation and he would buy it. Even if he still had doubts.

On some occasions, Maria would come home with red raw knees and messy hair and tell Mark she fell on the carpet in the bar. Other times, she would come home with a huge love bite on her neck, and she would tell him it was where the strap of her handbag had been rubbing it. On one occasion, he came home from work early to find her in the bedroom with another man, both of them down to their underwear. She dismissed it and made him believe that they'd spilled a fizzy soda drink all over them and were getting into some dry clothes. Now from an outsider's point of view, it seems pretty obvious that she was lying and did so frequently, but this is where the "love is blind" theory comes in. We want to believe people. Even more so if we love them or are close to them. Mark wasn't completely stupid, but his biases made him believe whatever lies Maria told him.

These biases are powerful things and can completely impair someone's ability to find the truth. Your brain goes into denial even when presented with the hard facts. Psychologists call this cognitive dissonance. A far-out and highly unlikely explanation is chosen over the unpleasant truth by biases in our brain over our gut feelings. These biases seem to override any form of rational thought, so as you can imagine, dealing with them can be quite an issue. (More on how to deal with your biases coming up later.) This is one of the biggest reasons why law enforcement agencies all over the world do not allow officers to have any involvement in a case that has any form of personal attachment. Their biases can cloud their judgement immeasurably. With that in mind, you will have to learn to put your biases aside when implementing your new knowledge and not allow them to prevent you uncovering the truth. This is much easier said than done.

Biases are by no means limited to spouses or family members either. A bias can begin simply because someone is like you, known as an affinity bias. This can be in physical appearance, personality, or even down to a singular possession they have that you own too, like a wristwatch, clothing brand, maybe even the fact that you both have tattoos or smoke the same brand of cigarette. We naturally look for similarities in people we like and dismiss anything that doesn't match our own preferences. Once one similarity has been established, the foundation to an affinity bias has begun, this can quickly lead to something called the halo bias. The halo bias is where you view a person as being a good person because they're like you. You wear the same clothes, have the same watch, you're from the same part of town, or went to the same school. They have these things in common with you so therefore they must be like you. That's the brain's way of sorting the new information it receives about a person. And because they're like you, they must be a good person, right? After all, nobody sees themselves as a bad person.

I'd like to mention here something called the Social Desirability bias. This is when a person is "socially desirable", in the sense that they are a popular and or attractive person (when I say attractive, that might not necessarily mean they are aesthetically pleasing to the eye to the point of being drop dead gorgeous, but at the same time not a fugly either). I'm not going to go down the route of superficial factors so much here as we are to look at the person generally being popular, desired and wanted. A person doesn't have to be the most gorgeous human specimen on the planet to be considered attractive. There are certain physical aspects that can highly increase their level of attractiveness, such as status, personality type, and so on. To clarify, when I say status it could be at the level of something like being a celebrity, which adds to the perceived value of a person's status. Have you ever noticed that an A-list actor or singer might be considered so much hotter than if that same person was working at a burger joint? There are certainly a few singers that I can think of that wouldn't get looked at twice if they were working as a janitor but get more bedroom activity than the Hilton hotel chain. So don't confuse socially desirable with beauty.

As we explore this area, realize that looks can still play an important role here too. According to the information gathered in The Pennsylvanian Study, (An Observational Study by JOHN E.

STEWART, 112 Mercyhurst College) at Pennsylvanian and Philadelphian courts, researcher's gathered data on 67 defendants. The defendants were a mix of black, Hispanic, and white, and there were 15 real judges in total. On average (mean), criminals of low attractiveness were sentenced to 4.10 years in prison, and criminals of high attractiveness were sentenced to 1.87 years in prison. This equals a 119.25% increase.

This tells us that socially desirable and good-looking people are not only more likely to receive lesser punishments than their not so lucky counterparts, but I have also found that they are also subject to an increased level of bias, of being believed when they make statements. I know it's an unfair world, but with the information in this book I will definitely help you to level the playing field.

On top of the previously mentioned desirability bias, there's also something called Halo bias. The halo bias, also known as the Halo effect, is a form of cognitive bias which impacts our overall impression of a person and influences how we feel and think about their character. Essentially, your general overall opinion of a person (he is nice) directly impacts all other areas of your evaluations of that person's specific traits (he is also smart), causing you to give credit to a person that might not be given to another, of whom you think less of. With all of that in play, we are also more likely to believe someone when the Halo bias is impairing our judgement. This bias can also be created simply with the trigger of yet another bias, the similarity bias.

Similarity bias (Also known as Affinity bias), is the tendency people have to connect with others who share similar interests, experiences and backgrounds. It doesn't stop there though. It can be triggered in many ways: if a person looks like you, sounds like you, wears the same type of watch or brand of clothing. The list goes on; the bias can be formed by two people simply driving or even liking the same kind of car. Any similarity a person shares with you, no matter how small, can create the foundation of a similarity bias. From there it can continue to grow, affecting your judgement upon that person. The more similarities that are found and highlighted, the more the bias is strengthened, which can then go on to create Confirmation bias.

I saw a great post on social media not long ago which read: "I Googled Confirmation Bias and it turned out to be exactly what I thought it was!" This is a perfect example of confirmation bias at work. It is what it says it is. It is any information, no matter how credible (or not as the case may be), that confirms your thoughts, feelings or suspicions. It is literally the tendency to search for, interpret, favor, and recall information in any way that confirms or supports our prior beliefs or values. At the same time, confirmation bias can tend to make us dismiss, or even outright ignore, any information and evidence that contradicts our beliefs, making us capable of being extremely one-sided in our arguments or beliefs and values too. The factor that impedes us even more is that confirmation bias can be strengthened the more information we receive, confirming our bias, and cognitive dissonance is appropriately increased in proportion to the confirmation bias, encouraging us to further conclude that our beliefs are correct. The dopamine hit you get when you think "I knew it" may be small, but it's certainly enough to make us want to recreate the same feeling. I can only speculate that there is a primitive need to feel right dating back to our tribal days. I have not come across any evidence or research to substantiate my speculation, but the concept seems a reasonable claim. Only in the sense that it would be a matter of life and death in that time to be either wrong or right. Maybe one day somebody will explore why there seems to be a deep natural evolutionary pressure to be correct. Current research seems to indicate that confirmation bias stems from reassuring yourself that you are coherent. We make a decision and look for evidence that our decision is correct, confirming our thoughts of ourselves as being rational human beings with the ability to apply logic. Let's face it, if we kept changing our minds every few minutes over what we thought was right we would appear incoherent to ourselves at the very least. Maybe this is why a trait of certainty in a man is so appealing to the opposite sex. It's possibly a survival instinct from our primal days yet again, but that's a topic for another book.

The kinds of biases we have looked into here can result in a phenomenon known as Belief polarization. As Mark Twain once said: "It is easier to fool and man than convince him that he has been fooled!" Which is especially true of anyone spending enough time cementing their beliefs and who is in a state of belief polarization. They could have only spent a short time, in comparison, convincing themselves or being convinced that the sky is green, yet you could spend enormous amounts of time bombarding them with evidence to the contrary and get nowhere. Even with the presence of irrefutable proof, their belief polarization will override rational thinking. The subject will be in deep denial, and cognitive dissonance will prevail in them still maintaining their beliefs. After all, they're a coherent and intelligent human, right? So anything challenging their beliefs and threatening that fact would ultimately mean that they're not so, therefore, no matter what the evidence is, it must be wrong. This is the reason people will continue to support certain beliefs, even after it's been proven they're incorrect.

In the past, people have been radicalized by religions or cults, and the deprograming process can be a phenomenal task. A person's bias can be so strong that having it undone can even lead to mental breakdowns. This same theory states that the strength of a bias can be just as stubborn in a belief that is recently formed as it can be in a belief that's been formed over years. In short, biases can be extremely powerful.

With all of this bias flowing through our system, is there anything else that could possibly make us even more vulnerable to our beliefs? Well, unfortunately, the answer to that is yes. Aside from the hundreds of different types of biases, some within others, there is also Truth bias.

We are naturally hard-wired with a Truth bias which is simply a bias to believe most people. Yes, contrary to what you might expect, truth bias is our default setting. We tend to credit people (even strangers) with the opinion that they're going to tell the truth. We may become skeptical of a person's story in due course, but we mostly lean towards giving everyone the benefit of believing them first until they give us a reason not to.

A useful little tip I feel I should squeeze in here is this; if you want to know what someone thinks of X, ask them how they think most people view X, their answer on how most people view X will tell you exactly how they view X.

For example: if you want to know what a person thinks of the current education system, you would simply ask them: "How do you think most people view the current education system?" This gives them the wiggle room to be truthful and give their opinion without being held accountable for it being *their* opinion. At the same time, if a person feels strongly about something and feels the need to express their opinion, they may respond with something like: "I don't know what most people's views are on the education system, but my feelings are..." Either way, it's a win-win. You get your answer no matter which way it comes out.

Memory distortion and polluted memories

This section is highly relevant for so many circumstances, it's unreal. You will see why as it unfolds. According to the latest research at the time of writing this, it's believed that each time we recall a memory it can cause minute changes that are barely detectable. On top of that little fact, each time we remember something, we're not actually remembering the event but accessing the memory from the last time we recalled it. So we're actually remembering the memory, not the actually event, and with each time we do this small changes happen, and it can cause the memory to become "polluted". This occurs because our retrieval system is not actually playing the memory back like a recording, but rather reconstructing it each time we attempt to recall the event from our memory banks.

An example here could be something like the following: Let's imagine that you take a long train journey over several hours late at night. The carriage you ride in has a slightly below average amount of commuters traveling at the same time, and the temperature is slightly cool. Later on you recall the journey, and you're asked how many people are on the train. You think back and reply that there weren't many people traveling at that time of night. A week later you're asked again and recall the memory once more, and as you do your subconscious edits it slightly. It knows there weren't many people on the train, so a few commuters "disappear" when your memory of the journey is replayed in your mind. Another week, and there's hardly anyone; a week or so more, and the train has become extremely sparse; yet more time goes by, and there are only one or two, then maybe just one other person, until eventually, you're the only person on the entire train. Over time, each occasion you recall the memory, your brain gives you the version you recalled last time, edited a little more by your subconscious mind on each occasion. Similarly, as the people on board the train thin out, the temperature could drop in your mind's version of events on each occasion too. Eventually, you could reach the point of it being abnormally cold on the train and you're sat there freezing and alone. The only person on the train for hours, late at night. Over a long period, this memory will seem unaltered to you, and you will swear that is exactly how it happened. Even in the event of a person showing you video footage of the event, just like in the biases above, you would find it hard to believe that you could be so wrong, when the memory of the event is so vivid and clear in your head. This is how two people can swear the other is lying as they tell a story of their version of events, which can appear completely different. Each of them swearing their version to be true. And to them, it is.

Memory distortion begins instantly and can even be influenced by external factors too. We will look into that a little here but first understand that this is the exact reason the police will attempt to get a witness statement as soon after the crime/accident as possible. They know that within minutes of the event that the brain can begin to distort the information they have received.

A research study was conducted in 1974 by psychologists Loftus and Palmer [4]

---

[4] [McLeod, S. A. (2014). Loftus and Palmer. Retrieved from https://www.simplypsychology.org/loftus-palmer.html]

Psychologist Elizabeth Loftus had been particularly concerned with how subsequent information can affect an eyewitness's account of an event.

Her main focus was on the influence of (mis)leading information, in terms of both visual imagery and wording of questions in relation to eyewitness testimony.

Loftus' findings seem to indicate that memory for an event that has been witnessed is highly flexible. If someone is exposed to new information during the interval between witnessing the event and recalling it, this new information may have marked effects on what they recall. The original memory can be modified, changed, or supplemented.

The fact that eyewitness testimony can be unreliable and influenced by leading questions is illustrated by the classic psychology study by Loftus and Palmer (1974), "Reconstruction of

Automobile Destruction" described below.

An experiment was conducted where participants watched a film about a traffic accident and were asked to estimate the speed of the cars, with different verbs including contacted, bumped, collided, and smashed. A week later, the participants were asked if there was any broken glass in the film. It was concluded that a word with a more forceful connotation led participants to believe that the speed of both cars was faster, and thus there's a greater chance that there was glass shattered in the accident. The use of the word 'smashed' insinuated there was but Elizabeth Loftus later reveals there was no sign of shattered glass in any part of the video.

Experiments have shown that even the word choices of the person asking about the memory can influence the witness's version of events. For example, asking a person, "was there much damage when the one car **bumped** into the other?" resulted in them recalling less damage being done in comparison to when asked "was there much damage when the one car **smashed** into the other?"

Many experiments on memory have been performed with similar results, demonstrating the fact that memories are easily distorted and polluted, sometimes by the person themselves, and other times by outsiders. Taking things a step further just to show you how easily it can be done, psychologists have even been able to perform studies where they have implanted a "false memory" in a subject, and it can be executed with ease (search for the *Lost in the Mall* experiment). It is surprisingly easy to implant a false memory in a person under the right circumstances, and with the right people reinforcing your suggestion. The repeated experiment can lead to the person going from being told and convinced it's real to telling others the story, and not only believing it to be true, but adding parts that weren't in the original implanted memory; the subject's mind adds and edits the story to what they believe works best. So not only does your mind pollute real memories, it also edits false ones in exactly the same way.

If you want an example of this, have you ever revisited the street you grew up on as a child? Or gone back to a school you attended years later? Only to find it's nothing like the way you remember it? Your logical part of your brain tells you this is the right place, but your memories differ from what you're seeing. It's surprisingly common and helps people relate to how easily memories can be manipulated over time. If the effect of time alone can distort the memories you have, imagine how easily other factors can have an influence. This is how couples can break up, and after years of being apart have two completely different stories of how the relationship went, yet both can believe they're telling the truth. Combine polluted and distorted memories with belief polarization and biases. and the person will be convinced that they're side of the story is the truth and anything else is an outright lie!

8. The Only two reasons people lie

After many years of studying deception detection, I've concluded that there are only two primary reasons why people lie. There may be many sub-categories of each, but from what I have found so far, these can usually be categorized as a sub-type of one of the two primary reasons. This is my opinion, and there is no evidence or scientific research to substantiate my thoughts, it's purely based on experience.

What are the two reasons, I hear you ask? They are simply Protection or Gain (sometimes both). People either lie to protect themselves or others, or they lie for gain. It may be financial gain, or simply to gain the upper hand in a social setting, but there's always a gain from the lie. Even in the extreme circumstance of the fact that the person is simply a compulsive liar, he is still gaining the feeling they get by telling the lies.

Let's look into it a little deeper. You tell a lie to your boss because you're late for work claiming the traffic was bad. You have just told a lie for protection and gain at the same time. You've protected yourself from the embarrassment of being yelled at by your boss, and at the same time, gained the opportunity to get straight on with your work and keep your job without explaining the real reason you are late.

You tell a lie to the police officer that's just pulled you over for speeding. You're protecting your license, protecting yourself from a fine, and protecting yourself financially.

You tell a lie to your friends to look popular. You gain social status (or so you think).

You tell a lie at a job interview. You gain a better job with improved career prospects.

So far, there's not a single example of a lie yet that I haven't been able to classify as being for protection or gain or even both. I'm interested to see if anyone can suggest one, but so far these two areas have covered the reasons behind every lie I have come across so far.

How is this helpful to you, though? Well, if you can narrow down the reason a person is lying, then build upon it, you can ultimately discover the person's drivers, which will help you get to the truth. We will cover this in more detail later.

Now that we have established the two primary reasons a person will lie, I think it's relevant to also explain how I categorize lies and reveal the three different types of lie that exist, and they are as follows:

1) Lies of commission.

"Did you steal my money?"

"No. I haven't touched your money." This is an outright lie.

2) Lies of omission.

"I don't even know where you keep your money." A lie of omission is more about what a person doesn't say, rather than what they do say. This is a lie more commonly used to avoid the guilt felt by a person of outright lie. They haven't said no, they have just left out some facts and steered the focus of the question away from the fact that they have stolen someone's money.

3) Lies of influence.

"You've known me for 20 years; I've looked after you and been there for you through thick and thin. I even bought you your first car." This is a lie of influence and the most powerful of the three. We will spend more time on this category because this style of lying is often missed by most people. The reason for that is, when done successfully, it tends to alter the way you perceive the person telling the lie and helps to influence your decision when it comes to the current subject being addressed.

This category also covers lies of embellishment, but we will explore that further when we have delved deeper into influence.

A few years ago, I frequently worked with a man called Darren who had a natural way of persuasion about him. He was truly a silver-tongued guy, and it was often said he could sweet talk the knickers off a nun. Looking back, the way he operated was in the very way I have described above. If he wanted to convince you to believe a lie, his method was very much a mix of what I have listed. If you asked him a simple question like:

"Did you take the extra boxes from the stores?" He would never give a simple answer of "No."

He would wrap his arm around you and guide you to a closed area where he took control of the conversation. He would then start with something like: "Let me tell you something." Then go on to explain all the good things he'd done throughout the day or week, finishing with something like: "Now do you really think I would have done all of that if I was going to take those boxes from the stores?"

Hindsight is a wonderful thing, and I can now see clearly that he regularly used to mix lies of omission with lies of influence. His lie of influence would be to convince you that, with all the good he'd done, there was no way he'd take the boxes or whatever it was you asked him about. This would be mixed with a lie of omission, because instead of answering your question, he'd get you to ask yourself if you thought he did it. After his influential speech had achieved its effect of causing doubt in your mind, this was enough to convince you that he didn't do it. He would never actually make an outright denial, therefore, committing a lie of omission instead.

Now that I've explained the three categories with examples, you will be able to determine which is which as we go on. We can start with denial. Once again, we can break denial down into two main areas. Nonspecific denial and overload denial. Here are examples of each:

Evasive (nonspecific) denial

So assuming that a simple question has been asked like, "Was it you who ate all my cookies?" And instead of the response being a simple "no", the person answers with something like, "I didn't do anything", or, "I wouldn't do a thing like that". Both of these are not specifically aimed at anything in particular and are very vague, therefore, they are really lies of omission and easily missed. When you ask somebody a question like this, listen carefully for the use of the word no. If you hear anything other than no, then you will more than likely need to investigate further. A yes or no question should always be answered with a yes or no, even if the person continues to talk after the initial yes or no, that's better than it not being there at all. With that being said, sometimes the person can say way too much after they have answered no, which neatly segues into the next section.

Overload denial

Using the same scenario as above, let's assume this time the person has answered "no" but then went on to give a long-winded response in great detail about how it would be impossible to have eaten your cookies, continuing to list all the apparent reasons why there was no way that they could have eaten them. In comparison to the severity of the question, the answer is extreme. If the answer seems way too long for the severity of the issue, then this should set alarm bells ringing and be considered a deceptive indicator. This kind of response can be delivered in several other ways too, which we will look at now.

Evasive or Reluctant Answers

I have sometimes asked a person a question and they appear to have not heard me, then go on to talk about a completely different subject. If this happens, ask again and wait for the response. If the same thing happens again, then approach from a different angle; this could be a sign of deception. On occasions, you can ask a question and get a response like, "I'm not sure I'm the right person to talk to about this", or even, "I'm not sure I can give you the right answer to that." Now these may be perfectly legitimate responses as they might actually not be the right person to talk to or may not have the answer, this is where your dynamic assessment will come in so pay close attention to their body language and demeanor.

During conversation, listen carefully and take into account that when a person is lying, they tend to give fewer details of things like time and specifics, location, and things they heard. When this is happening, you can increase the cognitive load for highly effective results (more on this later). When a person is telling the truth they can simply answer without the thought process involved of the ramifications of their answer, whereas when a person is lying, they need to answer strategically. This not only increases the cognitive load but the stress they're feeling too. The raised stress level will in turn result in more tells being displayed via their body language or speech, giving you the advantage to spot them.

Not understanding or repeating your question

This might sound like an obvious one, but you'd be surprised how many times it's missed. Now I have to stress yet again, there is no singular indication of a lie, so remember to look for clusters, because on its own this may not be a sign of a lie. It could be simply that the person didn't hear or may believe they misheard you, etc. Or it could simply be something a person does out of habit. So as I said, look for the groupings of tells. Repeating the question back, though, is a sign of deceptive behavior, so if spotted with others it will make the percentage chance of deception a lot higher. It allows a person who is being deceitful to buy themselves a little thinking time, and with thoughts moving a lot faster than speech, those valuable few seconds might be all they need to fabricate a story or alibi. Along with the person repeating the question back, another huge signal of deception is failure to understand a simple question. Especially when the content of the question is completely obvious.

Example: Your teenage son comes home and you ask a simple question like,

Q: "Did you break the handle on the refrigerator?"

A: "What refrigerator?"

Now let's leave out the possible scenarios where they live in an appliance store or something crazy and assume for the moment that, like most ordinary families, they live in a house where there is only one refrigerator. The supposed inability to comprehend the question is a definitive HPI of deception, but again, you should still implement the grouping rule and be looking for clusters of deceptive behavior.

Answering without answering.

It may seem a little obvious but similar to the above where the question is repeated to buy time, the question is responded to with an answer like,

"That's a good question."

"I'm glad you asked me that."

"Ah, just what I was expecting you to ask."

… And so on. Which is again very similar to the next verbal signal, where an evasive answer is given to the question. So instead of an outright "no", you might find the answer to be something like,

"Not that I remember."

"Not as far as I know."

"I can't recall."

"To my knowledge."

Again, these are all ways to skirt around the actual outright answer and give a response close enough to what the person wants to hear, in order to achieve the desired results. It's not an outright "no" and allows wiggle room if they're called out on their lie. Being able to respond with,

"Really? I wasn't aware." Or "I didn't say no, I said not that I remember."

Once again, these responses give way to the deep desire of a person not actually wanting to lie and alleviate the feeling of guilt, all the time allowing the person to misguide from the truth. I know I have mentioned this many times already, but I can't stress enough that these kinds of responses alone are not definitive signals of a lie. One brick doesn't make a wall. You are looking for several indicators that when combined increase the chances that the person you are talking to is being deceptive.

The Intelligence Trap

I have seen this one used so many times, and it never fails to amaze me how many people fall for it so frequently. Nobody likes to be thought of as stupid, and so when their intelligence is questioned, it causes them to go into a highly defensive mode.

Imagine a scenario where a person named Mick is talking to an associate, John, about ammunition for example, and says:

"You would have to be an idiot to think that 5.56mm rounds are any different from .223, they're exactly the same. The same size, same dimension. Only a complete and utter moron would think there's any difference."

John, not knowing what the difference is, agrees rather than look stupid in front of Mick. People don't like to look or feel less intelligent by a lack of knowledge. Salesmen use this to their advantage to 'upsell' all the time. When selling a car, they might say things like:

"Only the morons go for the base model", or "Any one with half a brain knows that the GLX is better value for money than the LX". Sometimes even blinding the poor unsuspecting customer with "science". Using Figures and numbers and mentioning horsepower and torque in ways the customer has absolutely no understanding of, in order to convince them to buy the higher priced model. The customer falls for it and spends more money rather than look stupid. Don't think it's always the general public either, I have even known judges to fall for it!

Anger as a response

I once took on a short-term assignment to provide close protection for a private client on a visit to Romania. He was only going to be there for a total of 4 nights and 5 days but wanted me to be present for a large cash transaction. There were a couple of hairy moments, but luckily at all went reasonably smoothly overall. After the exchange had been concluded, we went for a well-deserved meal and a couple of drinks (water for me). It wasn't long before my client (whose name I shall keep a secret but for the purpose of the book let's call him Rob), wanted to go for a massage. I have no problem with him doing whatever he wants, after all, I was only there to provide security for him at the point of the business transaction, but I still remained professional and escorted Rob to his destination. Everything went smoothly and the trip overall was a success. Upon returning to London however, Rob was only home for a matter of minutes before his wife asked him if he'd had a massage. At this point, I was expecting Rob either to say, "Yes, just a quick massage before we left." Or "No, I just did the business deal and came home." I was shocked when he suddenly began yelling and shouting with rage at his wife, exclaiming how she was always accusing him of things he hadn't done and verbally attacking her. Needless to say, as soon as the chance presented itself, I excused myself and drove home. After all, I had done my part and the last thing I wanted was to be dragged into someone else's domestic dispute. The point is, Rob denied having a massage when, in actual fact, he had gone for one, but instead of simply saying "no," he became aggressive in his response. Yet another HPI.

Playing down the issue

In a situation where a group of people are attempting to get to the bottom of an issue, a guilty party might try and play it down a little

148

with statements like; "It's a lot of fuss over nothing if you ask me." Or "Why is everyone so bothered about it?" This move to diminish the importance can even go as far as an attack on the process of trying to get to the truth. Possibly insinuating the whole thing is a "witch hunt" or even trying to sabotage the process by clouding people's judgment, again going back to lies of influence.

Absolutes

This is when a person responds with phrases like; "I never" or "I always". If a person doesn't generally use these absolutes in their speech, then they are to be treated as potential indicators of deception. Pay very close attention to them. Likewise, with "a million/billion percent" or "a thousand percent". The word "absolutely" itself is one of the absolutes that should ring alarm bells. Think about it like this, if someone asked you: "Do you want a cup of coffee?" and you didn't really want one, you wouldn't respond with: "Absolutely not!" alternatively, if someone asked you: "Hey, were you working last weekend?" again you wouldn't answer with "Absolutely!" the very thought of it seems absurd. The reason for this is the word "absolutely" is a highly expressive word used to drive home a feeling of, well, absoluteness. This is why it's so powerful, and why people use it as a convincer to attempt to persuade you that their answer is genuine and believable. There is a section later on where we explore convincing versus conveying when it comes to information and deception in more depth, but for now, we will continue to look deeper into the layers of deception.

Indirect denial

Depending on the situation, I have known instances where people have not directly lied but led a person to believe they have or haven't done something, by allowing them to form their own conclusions. Usually through sarcasm or an answer with a simultaneous sarcastic expression. For example:

Mother: "Did you lock the front door after you left the house?"

Son: "What do you think?" (Using a cynical tone and flashing a sarcastic glance)

This is another situation where the son isn't directly lying, he has answered in a way that leaves it to the mother to draw her own conclusions. Another example is if the answer goes something like this:

"No, I left it open so the whole neighborhood could come in and sniff your panties before they loot the place!"

It might seem a bit extreme, but this is the typical type of sarcastic answer a teenager might respond with if they want to cover a misdeed. They might not be lying, they might just simply not remember if they did or didn't lock the door, so they use the answer that saves them the most hassle. Again, it's not just the answer that tells you if they are lying or not so remember the Groupings rule here.

Convincers

There are two types of convincers, evasion convincers and influential convincers. The first – Evasion convincers- are when a person uses terms like:

- Probably

- More than likely

- Mostly / Most of the time

- Basically

- The majority of…

.. And so on. I'm sure you get the idea. For instance, a person being asked if they're coming to a party on Friday night might answer with:

"Yeah, it stands a good chance I'll be there." With that kind of answer, I'd assume that there's a better chance that they won't!

The answer again is not a direct lie, and once more provides the comfort that people seek from guilty feelings they have deep down when not telling the truth. It gives the impression that they'll attend the party to pacify the person asking and stop them probing further, yet they're still not committing to an actual "yes".

The second convincer is the Influential convincer. This generally comes in the form of a verbal reassurance of sorts. This is an attempt to influence your reception to their lie before they've even told it. For example, a person might start their sentence with:

- If I'm being honest

- To tell you the truth

- To be perfectly straight with you etc.

There are probably plenty more examples, but I'm certain I don't need to list them all. Again, I must stress that you keep in mind people's speech patterns and habits etc. and always apply the Grouping rule. I have recently been working with a Kurdish guy from Northern Iraq and he frequently starts a sentence with "To be honest with you…" In this instance this example wouldn't apply. It would only be if the person doesn't normally use this kind of speech, and it is mixed with other deceptive indicators. I know I've mentioned this a multitude of times but without implementing this rule, these tells are nothing. You must get two or more within a reasonable time frame to identify deception.

An area I frequently get called in to perform for certain clients on occasions is Perimeter Testing. On one occasion, though, I had a call from a private client who wanted me to test the security of his country home, a huge country house that he was extremely proud of. He had heard of me through a recommendation and invited me to join him to talk about his requirements. I explained that for a predetermined fee, I would essentially enter his house at some point within the next 10 days and write a full report on where his security flaws were and how they could be improved. The client, whom I shall call Cliff, was mostly happy, and I told him I'd call him the day after the job was done. One of the requirements, however, was for me to leave a greetings card on his desk as proof that I had in fact gained access to the property and not just made up a list of security improvements with the use of a pair of binoculars. I agreed to his terms and a formal typed agreement was printed and signed by both of us, and the process began.

A grand total of four days later a thank you card was left standing in the center of his desk, signed by me with a note saying "please call me" also written inside. After three days, I hadn't heard from Cliff, so I decided to call him. When I asked him why he hadn't called, he responded with:

"To be perfectly honest with you, I'd actually forgotten about the whole thing until you rang."

Which you don't have to be Sherlock to know was a complete lie. Nobody hires a man to break into their home and forgets about it. Furthermore, when I asked him about the card, he said he'd not found it and wasn't even sure if I'd ever even completed the task, essentially accusing me of being the one who was lying. Giving Cliff the benefit of the doubt and contemplating all manner of possible scenarios, like the cleaner moving the card etc., I agreed to do the whole thing again and arranged a meeting with him the following afternoon.

As I'd previously done the reconnaissance and was going to use the same method of entry, I could cut down the time frame and, with the whole operation being fresh in my head, I was confident that I could be in and out quite rapidly. I did the whole thing so quickly that night that I impressed even myself. I left another greetings card on his desk, only this time I made a small addition to my visit.

The following afternoon I attended my meeting with Cliff in the very office in which I'd placed the greetings card. He denied ever having received the card, yet again and I could tell he was being deceitful but to top it all, he was still implying that I hadn't completed my side of the deal, as there was no evidence. I simply smiled as I sat back in my chair, saying,

"I thought you might say that, so if you unlock your top desk drawer and look inside, you'll find, on page 179 of the novel you're reading, a secondary greetings card that I put in place for just such an occurrence." Giving him a moment to unlock his drawer and open the book to find my card, I continued with, "My report and invoice will be in the post." I then left Cliff open-mouthed and bewildered in his office staring at a "sorry for your loss" card, with absolutely no doubt that I had done what I had been requested to do.

Listen to what isn't there

We touched on this earlier, but I said we would cover it in a little more depth later on, so here we go. For this method you need to ask close-ended questions. They are simple and to the point. Like:

"Did you cheat on me last night with someone else?"

Listen carefully for the word "no". If you don't hear it straight away, that alone should raise some red flags. More importantly, though, you need to listen for the word "well", because if a person starts their reply to a close-ended question with the word "well", then they're more than likely lying to you. A person starting a sentence with the word "well" or "so" is giving you a HPI signal of deception, yet again though, it needs to be compared to their normal speech patterns. If they normally start a sentence with the word "so" then it can't be considered a signal of deception. As I said at the beginning, baselining plays a huge role, and congruency is key.

Another aspect to be taken into consideration here is this: If a person replies to an open-ended question with the word "well", then it stands a chance that they are simply just gathering their thoughts. If you ask them how their trip away was and they give an answer like: "Well, I suppose it was okay, considering the time of year." Then that would be fine. Ask them questions like: "Did you steal classified information?" Or "Did you cheat on your test?" And they answer with the word 'well', then they're more than likely lying to you, because they're now thinking about how they are going to answer your question and how to present their fabricated version of events. Put another way, they're deciding the best way to lie to you. The context can change everything, so you need to take all these areas into consideration.

How to use How

Using 'How' questions can be extremely effective when you listen carefully to the answer. For example, a woman might ask her husband: "How was Lucy last time you saw her?" And the husband replies with: "Lucy was typing up a report on her laptop." The answer was with *what* Lucy was doing and not *how* she was doing. This little inconsistency can be a key indicator of deceit.

Verbal Validation

This goes into the area of convincing again, and there is more to come on convincing as it's a very powerful tool. Verbal validation is a technique of priming you, prior to their statement, to believe that they are being truthful from the beginning. They are tools used by a person in an attempt to stop you in your tracks from even questioning the lie. They will use statements where a person swears upon their lie and might say something like:

- I swear on my children's lives.

- I swear on my mom's life

- I swear on my grandmother's grave

But more often than not, usually invoke religion, with phrases like:

- I swear to God

- As Allah is my witness

- God knows it's the truth

- I swear on the Holy Bible

This is an extreme but very effective way of convincing you they're telling the truth, because let's face it, you have nothing that trumps God! So be aware of this very persuasive method when it comes to getting you to surrender. It works more often than you would expect.

Do I need to remind you to look for clusters again here, or are you getting it yet?

Convincing Vs. Conveying

Remember earlier when we spoke about lies of influence and how powerful they can be? Well, this is the part where we revisit that area and delve deeper into the way people use "inducers" to cover their lie and get you on side to believing their story.

A way to explain this is: liars try to convince you they're telling the truth, whereas honest people simply convey the information you need, after all they don't need to convince you of anything if they're innocent, they just need to give you the facts. A liar, though, feels the need to convince you of their innocence and this is where you need to pay close attention to what is being said and ask yourself: "Are they giving me the facts or are they trying to convince me that they're not guilty of anything?"

Let's create a scenario where you are at work and some money is missing from the petty cash. You ask a colleague if they've taken any cash from the tin. An honest person would most likely answer with a simple "no." the reason is, that's the single most important fact that they need to deliver. They may follow on with questions like, "Have you asked Sue?" Or "Did you check the drawer?" etc. but that's simply human nature. Whereas a guilty person might or might not have the "no" within their response, because of the simple fact that they are indeed guilty and will feel the need to convince you of their innocence. Instead of a simple "no" this need will often emerge in statements like:

- I wouldn't do something like that

- Do you think I would risk my job over a bit of petty cash?

- Ask anyone, they'll all tell you, I'd never take a penny

- What kind of a person do you think I am?

- I'd never do anything of the sort

When it's pointed out to you, it's very easy for you to think that all this is very obvious, but I can assure you that these powerful and convincing statements are frequently missed. Even by the best! I have been on the receiving end of these type of statements more times than I care to recall, they are extremely convincing to anybody!

And that's what makes them so powerful. The reason behind why they are so convincing is that it's the type of statement that you might catch yourself making, and therefore logic makes it reasonable for you to believe what you are being told. The main difference is that an innocent person would make a singular convincing statement with a reasonable explanation made up of factual evidence or reasoning. They are at this point just conveying the information they feel you need. A guilty person, however, would simply reel off a stream of convincing statements, because that's all they have on their side.

The lack of evidence means they cannot produce facts to prove their innocence and, therefore, have to use whatever is left in their arsenal to convince you. It stands to reason that if they can't prove they're not guilty, they need to convince you they're innocent. These same statements have duped professional law enforcement officers interviewing criminals, so I can assure you that unless you are going to employ the systems you have learned from this book, they'll more than likely dupe you too!

Now that you have these extremely powerful methods and techniques of spotting deception, you must remember two important things, one is the Grouping rule that I keep bringing up (you need to look for clusters and deviations from a person's baseline) and the second is that you actually use it. The knowledge itself is useless without the application. It's not easy to master, but you'll find once you get used to it, it will start to become second nature. Until you find yourself using it without even realizing you are. When you get to this level of unconscious competence you will have really mastered the world of lie detection, and it will open your eyes to reveal exactly how many lies get told to you and how often!

The Law of Reciprocation

During my time working as a freelance investigator, I learned about the law of reciprocation. The theory is quite simple; if you do something for somebody, the more inclined they will be to do something for you. There was a case of a salesman working on an auto sales lot who had higher sales than any of his fellow employees. His trick was simple. On a hot day (which it often was in Arizona), he would approach a potential buyer and briefly introduce himself. Midsentence he would stop in his tracks and say: "You look like you're getting hot, let me grab you a soda." He would then go over to the vending machine and using money from his own pocket buy a can of Pepsi and run back and give it to the potential customer. After handing it over he would simply politely excuse himself, saying if they needed anything at all, his name's Hal, just give him a shout, and he will do whatever he can.

Most of the time, when the customer was ready to make a purchase, they would seek out Hal and even if other salesmen offered assistance, the customer would decline and continue to search until they found Hal to close the deal.

The reason for this is simple. The small act of buying them a soda invoked the law of reciprocation. Hal had done them a favor by purchasing a soda for them on a hot day, so they wanted to return the favor by dealing with the salesman who had shown them the act of kindness. His sales were the highest, and he was the most successful salesman that the car lot had ever employed.

The reason I mention this is you need to be aware of the subtle, and sometimes very small acts, that are performed in an attempt to influence your perception of the person you are questioning. Even a small gesture like offering a sweet or gum can be an indication of somebody attempting to convince you of what a good, moral, and honest person they are.

Sometimes they're just offering you gum because your breath smells.

Pause Rate

Think of a question to ask your subject but before you do, think about how you would answer if you were asked the same question.

For example:

If you were asked what you had for dinner 3 nights ago, you'd usually need to stop and think about it wouldn't you? (I say usually to allow for things like special occasions or the fact that a person has a set routine of pizza for dinner every day). So, assuming the subject has a more varied palette, or it wasn't their birthday, they would normally have to stop and think for a moment. If they instantly remember facts, then this is a sure sign of rehearsal. Meaning the person has practiced what they're going to say, and that is usually a huge sign of a lie. Think about it, how many times have you heard things in movies like, "You better think about what you're going to tell the police when they get here."? People have no need to think about what they're going to say if they're reciting the truth, they just say what happened. People hiding the truth though, the ones who are lying, have to rehearse what they're going to say first. Therefore, if it seems rehearsed then it's more than likely a lie.

Clunky speech

What I mean by this is when a person isn't speaking smoothly. They speak then suddenly stop and continue and throw in a few fillers ("erm") too. The reason they do this is that they are in mid-sentence and realize they're about to say something they shouldn't. So they cut themselves off and quickly try to say something else. There can be so many reasons for this, nervousness, fear, etc. So always take the context into consideration. Sometimes people have to think about how they're going to answer purely because of the circumstances. Telling a story amongst friends, can come out completely differently when the same story is being told in a public speaking scenario. They may demonstrate clunky speech in this instance, even if it's a story they've told many times before. The time it should be ringing alarm bells is if a person is giving an explanation and their statements are flowing smoothly, but when you question an inconsistency the clunky speech begins.

The Quicksand Effect

As I mentioned, unless you're consciously using the knowledge you've learned, it is of no use to you at all. So you must train your brain to change the way it takes information in. This shift in the way you make yourself perceive information is referred to by the CIA as going into L-Squared mode. It's far from easy and can be quite taxing to start with, and you'll find that you seem to unconsciously switch it off. Train yourself to fight this and keep it going. It won't be long before you've got it down to a fine art. Push past the pain zone and persist, just like you would at a gym to build your body, do the same to build your brain. With enough practice, you'll be on your way to the point where that big holographic indicator may as well be flashing above a person's head for you to see every time you detect deceptive behavior!

When I first learned this method, it was intended for use professionally. It wasn't long, however, before it spilled over into my personal life (even as I was learning it) and soon, every area of my life. I have found myself becoming so used to it, I started at one point forcing myself to 'switch it off'. I have since found a happy medium where it's now another tool in my toolbox for me to utilize should I require it.

Of course, I didn't create the method; I'm just presenting it to you in a bundle of systems used to detect deception. As I mentioned earlier, I've primarily worked as a freelance contractor most of my adult life (as well as one or two other jobs here and there). I've been lucky enough over the years to have worked with some absolutely outstanding people and, at the same time, some complete numpties too. As much as I'd love to rattle on about the amazing guys I've had the privilege of meeting and working with, it's the numpties that are always good for one thing: a good story.

Most people have heard of the world-famous British SAS (Special Air Service), however, there is another branch of the British Special Forces that is lesser known, called the SBS (Special Boat Service).

I'm one of a lucky few that has had the pleasure of working with and being friends with guys from both, and I cannot stress enough how they're almost like a different breed. It's not something I can quite describe and do justice to, but I can tell you, that I have the highest of admiration for these guys and what they do and have done. Anyway, when I moved from Arizona back to England for a while, I took on a stop gap job with a local security company. I wasn't there long before I got to know most of the guys and came across one person in particular who seemed to be the talk of the company. I'm not going to reveal his name but for the purposes of this book and a couple of other reasons I'm going to refer to him as Kermit!

Kermit claimed to be former SBS. Now it's very seldom that I judge a book by its cover, but I was pretty certain he wasn't. Although one of the things he seemed most proud of was his blue faced Omega Seamaster which he claimed was issued to him by the SBS.

Most of the time, SBS. guys start their career off in the Royal Marines. There are an odd few who don't start this way, although it's extremely rare. Now this is where things didn't seem to add up. Kermit claimed that before he was SBS, he in fact spent 12 years as a sniper for the RAF (Royal Air Force). Needless to say, I was exceptionally skeptical at this point. Even though most of the staff there had him down as a Walter Mitty, nobody could actually prove what he had or hadn't done.

Eventually, curiosity got the better of me and I called a friend who was former SBS (and whose name I certainly won't be revealing) and asked him if he'd heard of Kermit. It was no surprise when it turned out that he, or any of his former colleagues had ever heard of Kermit. When the Omega Seamaster inevitably came up in conversation, my friend told me to look at the back of it. If it had the SBS insignia on the back then there was at least a small chance of some truth in his claims, however, if it was not there, then he was almost definitely telling lies about his past.

Armed with this new piece of intel, I waited until the next shift when we were all working together, and Kermit started gobbing off about his adventures in the Special Forces and flashing his Omega around. I asked him for a closer look, and he handed me his prestigious Swiss watch that seemed to be made in Taiwan, and, just as I expected, there was no SBS badge on the back. I handed it back to him and mentioned the little fact of the missing insignia. After a roll of verbal stumbling, he boldly announced that of course it was missing and that he wasn't stupid enough as to carry the original on him; that one was locked in his safe at home, and he wore this copy as a representation of the Original Omega due to the fact that the original was way too valuable to risk losing by wearing it daily.

The point to all of this is knowing that someone is telling lies and getting them to open up and tell the truth are two different things altogether. The knowledge that someone is being deceitful is only half the battle. It's all well and good knowing someone is lying, but calling them out on it only creates resistance.

For example, if you were to ask someone, "Did you eat my cookies?" and they denied it while you know for a fact that they did, most people would continue down the path they started and follow up with

"Are you sure you didn't eat them?" This persistence to accuse will only result in the person standing their ground and becoming more stubborn in their answer.

It's very much like quicksand, the more you struggle against it the deeper into it you get. People in the middle of a lie will not change their answer, irrelevant of how many times you repeat the question. It's not like there's a magic number and the response will alter when you hit it.

"Oh shucks, you asked me for the fourth time, you got me, I wasn't expecting that, okay I ate your cookies."

It sounds absurd when I put it like that, yet it seems to be a method that so many people try, and I myself have even been guilty of it before learning the systems within this book.

That being said, three seems to be the magic number when someone fails to answer the question entirely. I have found that if a person has evaded a direct answer to the question three times, then that is a huge HPI of a lie and it should be further investigated.

Telling the Truth with Lies

Intelligence officers are what's known as the "boots on the ground" and are the specialists in gathering HUMINT which is the term used for Human Intelligence. There are many other forms of intelligence such as SIGINT for Signals Intelligence, IMINT for Image Intelligence, or COMINT for Communications Intelligence, and so on. One of the unofficial terms used frequently within the

Intelligence Community or I.C. is RUMINT, which is the term used for Rumor Intelligence. This is basically the gossip that goes around and, although it is in no way official, it's usually more reliable than official sources.

Although it can work the other way too and turn into Chinese whispers. The reason I bring this up, though, is because sometimes people can lie without realizing they're lying. For example: imagine a situation where you're at work and Tracy from your department asks if your colleague, Bob has a criminal record. You don't know so you ask a friend. The friend makes a mistake, getting Bob confused with another member of staff and says "yes". You then go back to Tracy and tell her that Bob does have a criminal record. Now, even though it's not true, Tracy is not lying when she's asked if Bob has a criminal record and answers "yes". I've seen this kind of thing happen countless times. So just because the information isn't true, doesn't mean that the person is lying. I only added this simply because this occurs more frequently than most people realize.

Persuading Vs Information

Earlier we talked about convincing versus conveying, and I said we will explore it more later on, so as promised, this is one of the areas that we will address in this section.

This one is a huge tell. When I stop and listen to someone's words analytically, this is the one that usually has more red flags than a Russian airport. As we discussed earlier, when a person is being honest, they simply convey information. They have the facts and, ultimately, the truth on their side. When a person is being deceitful, however, they don't, so they have to convince you that they're telling the truth. Listen carefully to what they say and ask yourself, "Are they giving me information or are they trying to convince me that they are telling the truth?"

Here are some more ways a person might try to convince you they're being truthful.

- Using statements like: "Ask Steve, he was there." This is not a conveyance of information; this is a method of trying to convince you. Whether someone else is there or not, it provides you with no further evidence in the way of facts.

- Guilt tripping – Asking questions like; "Why am I being singled out?" Or "Why aren't you interrogating anyone else?" And "Why are you interrogating me?" This is an attempt to change the approach the person is taking and back off a little using sympathy or guilt as a tool.

- Using history – Using phrases like; "Last time this happened you thought it was me then too, but it turned out you were wrong." Or "We've been through this type of thing before, and it always turns out to be somebody else." Just because it wasn't them last time doesn't mean it isn't them this time, so treat each case individually.

- Deflecting blame – this is when a person attempts to move themselves out of the frame by putting another person in it. They might say something like; "Try asking Adrian, he's the one who's been caught stealing from his last two jobs." In this instance you can simply make a mental note of the name mentioned and reply with something like "I can ask Adrian his version of events later, but right now I'm asking you." And don't distract yourself from the case in hand. Stay focused and continue your line of questioning.

- Self-deprecation – This is when a person deliberately downplays themselves in an effort to make themselves appear less capable and weak. The officer asks them: "Did you hack into the computer system?" And the subject replies with: "Oh come on, I'm not that smart, I can just about use my cell phone." This is an attempt to make himself look less intelligent than he really is. Another huge red flag.

As you can imagine, there are a multitude of ways a person might try to influence your thought patterns but the examples above give you some idea of what to look for. This knowledge will hopefully be able to assist you in staying on track for when it comes to identifying deception and moving on to extract a confession.

Whilst listening carefully to the response a person makes verbally, here are a few areas for you to watch and pay attention to as the subject is talking, that may be displayed while you question them.

The first one is known as lip compression. There are never absolutes when it comes to body language and nonverbal cues. The following, however, are actions that you can say with almost 100% certainty are translatable into what they mean. For example, lip compression is a sign of withheld opinion. I'm sure you've seen the popular pictures online of politicians performing the action. Remember, it's not necessarily a lie but almost definitely withheld opinion when you see a person tightly pressing their lips together.

Staying in the same region, when a person places something into their mouth, it's almost certainly a need for reassurance. This can be anything from a finger to a pen or even hair. With the exception of being used for seduction, placing something into the mouth is a natural form of pacification, going back to when they're a baby and are given a pacifier, or suck their thumb, and so on. In adults it's more subtle, but a pen or finger between the teeth, or long hair pulled around the front of the face and slid between the lips, is a sure sign of a need for reassurance. A very useful tip for people in sales: if they see a customer doing this at the point of addressing a certain topic then that is definitely an area to revisit and address that customer's needs.

Fidgeting is another area that can give a lot away about a person's frame of mind. In a high stress scenario, fidgeting can be a sign of an adrenalin rush, and that energy needs to go somewhere. With this dump of adrenalin, if the person is confined to a room or a chair, they might start to bounce the knee around or become extremely restless as a method of energy expenditure. A person will get this adrenalin rush when going into what's commonly known as flight or fight mode, so when they're able to do neither, the extra energy has to go somewhere. This is when you get the leg bouncing up and down or someone might pace or fidget to burn it off. Of course, the adrenalin rush came from somewhere, so if you're interviewing them for a crime and it happens after the revelation of a particular piece of evidence, then you can look deeper into why they were affected by the evidence produced, the question asked, or the statement made.

Hopefully this section has given you more of an insight of the types of lies there are, the reasons people may tell them, and some of the methods people use to lie and evade telling the truth. This new information should serve you well but remember, sometimes you will get what you look for. Even the professionals have made mistakes. In the next section we're going to explore how you can misread the sign and how easy it is to make mistakes when it comes to lie detection.

9. Misreading the Signs

This section is extremely vital in respect of most of the areas we've covered so far. Whether it's clunky speech, body language, or any other aspect of deception detection, they should always be subject to dynamic assessment. You should always be questioning what I call external variables. These are influencing factors that need to be taken into account because of how they might affect the subject. For example, we covered the differences between being open and being closed off and demonstrating a closed posture, but could the person you're talking to simply be cold? Are they injured? Are there any inhibitors in their system, such as drugs, medication, or alcohol? There are so many more factors to take into consideration, and we will not only explore some of them in this section but also how easily they can be missed or misread.

I was called in to assist on an investigation a few years ago that was yielding no results despite 3 suspects being questioned with no developments. It was taking some time to get anywhere for the investigating officer, and progress seemed to have hit a plateau. He'd started this whole investigation in late December, and it was now well after the Easter holidays and he'd become seriously frustrated. It was time to call in the experts. He sent me several video recordings of the suspects during their initial, secondary, and most recent interviews. The first interviews were short to establish basic facts; the second interviews went a little deeper, but the third ones really probed. It was at this point I thought I had hit the jackpot. When asked about certain events, a particular female, whom I will refer to as Sally (not her real name), would cover her mouth when answering. She'd bring her hand up and rub her nose. Going back to the first interview which wasn't as probing, she hadn't done this action once. I was convinced she was covering something up. When spending more time looking for cues of deception, I convinced myself they were there. I called my friend and asked him to make arrangements for me to interview Sally in person.

I was geared up and ready to go on the morning of the interview. It was a lovely sunny day; I was feeling fresh as a daisy and everything was going well. I was going to get a confession then enjoy the rest of the day celebrating in a beer garden with a little liquid refreshment until sunset. What could possibly go wrong?

I waited patiently, and when given the nod that she was in the interview room, I walked in and my heart sank. My mistake hit me straight away. There she sat, more than a little frustrated at being called in again, but what stood out the most was her prominently red nose. I sat with her for a few seconds and established that her sinuses give her terrible grief when the pollen count goes up, and she can't help but constantly rub her nose when it irritates her. Of course, this hadn't happened in the initial interview because it was done in December, and the pollen count was low. By the time of the third interview, the weather had begun to change, and pollen count had risen. This is when she had started to rub her nose frequently. Today, even though it was a beautiful sunny day for me, the pollen count was through the roof and was hell for her. Obviously this changed everything.

I had seriously misread the signs. I had convinced myself other signs of deception were visible after seeing her rub her nose and cover her mouth so many times during the third interview that I ignored all other signals and was only looking for deception. This just goes to show how easily the signs can be misread, even by professionals. This event did of course act as a learning experience for me too. It helped to demonstrate how easy it is to look for something and convince yourself it's there, and of course how easily your biases can be triggered once you do.

As it happens, it turned out to be none of the original three suspects but somebody completely different, just in case you were curious.

This particular event was one which was influenced by external factors, but I have had other experiences that have ended with a similar result from something less obvious.

I won't go into the full explanation, but the person I was interviewing had eaten a rather hot curry the night before and was showing all the signs of discomfort during the interview. Signals that I had started to receive as possible guilt were actually signals that he needed to run to the rest room rather urgently. He couldn't wait for the interview to be over so he could run and get relief as the pressure mounted with the questions. Luckily, he managed to make it in the nick of time and didn't end up in the… well let's just say he wasn't actually guilty of anything and avoided any potential accidents too.

These examples are extreme cases, but in so many instances you will get what you look for. If you look for signs of deceit, you will find them. I'll say it again; you get what you look for. Pareidolia is the tendency to perceive specific and frequently meaningful images in a random or ambiguous visual patterns. The scientific explanation is the human ability to see shapes or make pictures out of randomness. Think of the Rorschach test, better known as the inkblot test. I have no doubt you have experienced similar occurrences yourself, an image in the shape of a cloud perhaps or face in a random rock formation. The list of examples could be endless; the point is if you look for a pattern in randomness, eventually you will find it. Just like deceit, if you look for it, you will find that too. The experts are the ones who can differentiate between when these cues are credible signals of deceit or just a random movement. The primary key is usually clusters. As I've mentioned before, this and other factors combined will give you the edge when it comes to spotting lies. It's not just about reading body language but all of the signs from voice, tone, the words that are spoken, body language, eye movements, breathing, and pulse rate, as well as deviation from the baseline, and more. That's the reason I compiled the methods into this book for you to learn in the order I wrote them. As you learn each discipline, eventually you will be able to put them all together and form the ability to spot deceit easily.

Gut Feeling

Intuition. Good old-fashioned intuition. In the intelligence world, operatives live by a set of rules known as the Moscow rules, one of which is always to trust your gut. Fear is a basic instinct, and we frequently begin to suspect something, even when there is no obvious reason to experience such suspicion or fear. Even today we have no scientific explanation for this, all that is known is your brain is subconsciously recognizing that fear or suspicion well before it has reached your conscious mind. The psychological term for this is "thin slices". Your subconscious mind can detect vast amounts of detail at a much more rapid rate than your conscious awareness can pick up on them. Researchers have found it can be as fast as 1/25 of a second. Within that "thin slice" of time, your subconscious mind has detected something that your conscious awareness has yet to register, and that is the reason why you sometimes get that gut feeling but don't know why.

10. Finding out the Truth vs. Confirming Suspicions

With what we've learned so far about biases and misreading the signs, there is one other area I feel I should address when it comes to the potential mistakes that can be made, one that I certainly learned my lesson with. If you ever find yourself in a position where you have to quiz somebody about a particular event, then the less you know from the beginning the better. I know this might sound counter intuitive, but believe me, information can sometimes be your enemy. It can create biases within you before you've started. Any information you need to know, you can ask from the person directly. Find out as you go. A big thick file of information and evidence, however, is good for one thing, but we will cover that in the section about confessions. Staying on track, the less information you have to start with helps you to remain as objective as you can from the beginning of the questioning. If you read a file packed with circumstantial evidence, or have a conversation with someone who projects their thoughts and feelings about the person on to you, then you can end up unconsciously forming a bias or belief about this person before you've even had the chance to establish if they are in fact guilty or not.

Many years ago, when I first started to investigate marital infidelity cases, I came across a perfect example of this very kind of thought pattern. I was hired by a lady who asked me to find out what her husband was up to. She told me all about his POL, or patterns of life, and the reasons for her suspicions. I had made my mind up; he was cheating, and I was going to prove it.

However with all of the information I'd got and everything I'd been told, I had made my mind up that this guy was cheating. The biases had already started to take root and I had convinced myself that this was the case. I had him under covert surveillance and watched closely, just waiting for the time to be right for me to get my proof. The first couple of days went by and though there were no shady motel visits, his actions did seem a little suspicious. His activities weren't lining up with what he was telling his wife. I watched and waited; maybe he was being careful or cancelling his plans at the last minute as a result of being over-cautious. Surely if I waited, the lady he was cheating with would show up at some point. Days later I still had nothing. Yes he was coming home late, but he was driving to see people all over the place on his way home. Not just one specific person but different people in different neighbourhoods. He was telling his wife he was at work when he was in fact out in the city center, but he was meeting with people in ways that seemed like casual meetings as opposed to any official business, but nothing that appeared to indicate an affair. What on earth was going on? This guy was definitely up to something, and I was determined to find out what it was. Then I followed him as he walked into a particular type of shop, and it all made sense. The secrecy, the lies the covering of his actions; all became perfectly clear.

I called his wife with the intention of getting the answer to one specific question. It was time to utilize my elicitation skills without arousing any suspicion. I disguised my inquiry within a few other questions about her personal details and a mixture of other snippets of information I pretended that I needed, and got the answer I wanted. Just as I thought, I confirmed my suspicion. It was her birthday coming up! He wasn't having an affair, he was arranging a surprise birthday party.

I continued to investigate purely to get 100% confirmation, which didn't take too long. Using highly effective elicitation skills I had developed in my training, I managed to talk to one of the invited guests and find out for certain what I had concluded.

I was just about to start patting myself on the back for a job well done when I then realized I had now inadvertently created a greater challenge: What do I tell his wife?

The lesson from all of this was; that I had been influenced by prior information. I had concluded that he was cheating before I had any actual proof. My decision had been influenced by nothing other than circumstantial evidence based only on suspicions. Had I approached this objectively and set out to find out what was actually going on rather than to prove he was cheating, I would have probably wrapped the whole thing up a lot faster. The experience gained from it, though, had taught me a lesson for the future.

11. What is said Vs. The way it's said - The Truth behind Voice Tone

The same sentence said with a different tone can have two completely different meanings. Just the words, "What are you looking at?" said in a different tone can be anything from an inquiry to the means of trying to provoke a fight. This can really help highlight how much of a difference tone plays in the real meaning behind what a person is saying. Of course, posture, expression, volume, and many other factors play a pivotal role too, and we will cover that in this section as well.

One of the things I have had to learn to live with in recent years is a problem known commonly as "Cocktail Party Deafness". Maybe I've fired a few to many gunshots indoors without ear protection. Maybe I've driven a few too many tanks without ear protection. Maybe I've been around a few too many explosions, or maybe it's genetic. I really don't know. Either way, it's something I'm coping with but has its drawbacks. In short, it means that I hear almost everything at the same volume no matter how loud or quiet it is. If I'm in a house with a washing machine spinning, a TV on, a clock ticking, and a person talking to me, I hear it all on the same level. I have to consciously attempt to single out the person's speech and ignore the other sounds. It can have its advantages, but most of the time, I find myself struggling to hear people and shouting above noises that other people can't hear. I've never looked too deeply into it or whether it can be resolved, but I do know other people who have had similar issues. The reason I bring this up is because sometimes you can be talking to a person, and if they can't hear you properly, they might be showing signals that are not their usual baseline self. On the opposite end of this, they could be talking quite loudly to shout above a noise you can't hear, but if you're unaware of it and that noise stops (like the washing machine reaches the end of its cycle etc.), then the person you are talking to might lower their voice. To you the event that caused the volume of their speech to lower might not immediately be apparent, so it can be easy to jump to a conclusion about the person's feelings towards a particular subject. Making a mistake when it comes to reading people is easily done, because you can never tell exactly what is going on for that person with 100% accuracy. This is a perfect example of external variables coming into play as we discussed in the last section.

An area I can say has been a huge indicator of deception to me has been something I call speech fade. This is when someone starts a sentence with conviction at appropriate or slightly above average volume and then slowly lowers the speed, tone, and volume of their speech until their voice fades away into not much more than a barely audible mumble. Now as we have just covered, there are always external variables that can come into play and dynamic assessment is always key, but speech fade is definitely an area I pay close attention to whenever it happens.

Another area to pay close attention to is pitch. A little helpful hint for the male readers here: if a female is attracted to you there will be a slight elevation in her pitch when she talks to you. Someone I know used to make regular Facebook live videos and would say hello to all the viewers as she started off. I was always complimented as she read out the names, and a slight smile would come to her face as she read my name an octave or two above the other names she called out. Now that you're aware of it, you can listen out for it when talking to the opposite sex. Of course, if you start talking to girls regularly and they all start talking to you in a voice tone that would rival batman, then perhaps you should consult a stylist.

For the female readers, I'm afraid I'm not sure if the same rule applies. Perhaps this would be a good area to research; I'd certainly be interested in your findings. Before I digress too much however, while we are talking about pitch, I'm going to cover where it comes into play with regards to deception. Listen carefully to a person when they speak, and if what they say is stated as fact with a pretty much constant tone, then this is what I would expect and consider congruent. On the other hand, if a person talks and their pitch changes towards the end of the sentence, making it more like a question than a statement, then I would certainly be asking myself why. This slight rise in pitch is indicative of uncertainty. They're not sure if you're buying into their lie. This is frequently accompanied with an eye brow raise, like a sort of visual display of them questioning if you believe them or not. It usually fades quickly if you continue without challenging what they're saying. Now that it's been highlighted to you, you might find you become more aware of people's speech and find this happens more frequently than you would expect.

This next observation is probably going to seem obvious yet happens so often I can't believe that so many people get away with it as often as they do. And that's crying without tears. I see it so regularly, in person, on TV on news reports, interviews, and even in court. Yet it gets missed by so many. A person giving an emotional speech as they tell their story might be making all the right noises, have the croaky voice and sniff as they talk, but if there's no actual tears coming from their eyes, then it's usually not real. I consider it a big indication of deceit, and it generally switches me to high alert to look for other signals of deception.

While we're talking about tears, I want to also mention a sign of potential deceit which I call "The Display Tear". This is when a person is crying for the camera, or maybe even their boyfriend/ husband or just generally want the sympathy vote and to win you over in their emotional game of influence. The Display Tear is when they have that single tear creating a line from the corner of their eye trickling down their cheek and they don't wipe it away. I'm sure everyone reading this book has cried at some point in their life and therefore knows full well that tears are annoying. I can also tell you from experience that no matter how upset a person is and no matter what the situation, people will wipe them away. Unless of course, they want them to be seen! Hence, The Display Tear.

Having lost friends, family, and loved ones over the years, I can tell you that wiping tears away is a natural occurrence. It's done automatically and without thought. It actually takes more thought to leave it there bugging you than to wipe it. Being through many different types of bereavement at different intervals of my life, I have never found myself in a position where I'm too upset to wipe away tears. I give it as little thought as scratching an itch. I do it unconsciously, just like everyone else. And just like everyone else, we all wipe tears away when we're upset unconsciously. So if a tear is left to make its way down a person's cheek, it's there because they want it to be seen and they want you to see how upset they are. It's a manipulative method of convincing you of their emotional state.

I will also add here that as a person is crying and talking; if they give a slight micro expression of a half-smile as they do, this is a signal that's come to be known as "Dupers Delight". It's the rapid forming of a smile that goes as quickly as it comes. It's a very rapid micro expression that's sometimes easy to miss. Be aware that a person doesn't have to be crying for this to happen. They can simply be telling their story and this half smile flashes for less than a second. It's an unconscious leakage of their real feelings. Their real feeling being that of delight that you seem to be believing their lies.

Although I mentioned it can be done when a person is not crying, it is easier to spot when they are. To know for sure if it's real or not, when a person is crying simply look at their mouth. It should be curling down at the corners. If it is, then it's more likely that the emotion is real, if it's not then it's almost certain that the emotion is false. If a person's lips are curling up at the corners as they cry, this is definitely a sign of incongruence and should be investigated.

12. The Choice Justification Pyramid

The Choice Justification Pyramid explains how one decision can result in a major action that feels justified by the subject.

Imagine a lady at work, let's call her Carol, Carol has worked hard all year and is expecting a bonus that has been hinted at throughout the year. A company meeting is arranged, and all of Carol's peers are given a hefty bonus and Carol is given a mediocre bonus at best. She feels rather dismayed after working harder than all of her peers at the fact that her efforts are not recognized. Let's say her peers each got a twenty-thousand-dollar bonus, and Carol got only got three thousand dollars. Carol, feeling a little annoyed and rather dismayed, goes back to her office and sits staring at her computer about to get back to work. She's in the middle of transferring funds to the accounts of the company's creditors and a thought enters her head. What if she transferred two thousand dollars to her own account?

At this point Carol is standing right at the apex of the Choice Justification pyramid. Here, we're going to metaphorically split Carol into two. Carol number 1 is going to come to the decision that she deserves the extra 2 thousand dollars, and nobody would notice. No great harm would be done, and it would compensate for her not getting as much as her colleagues. Carol number 2 decides, as tempting as it is, that it's wrong, and her job and integrity are worth more than a couple of thousand dollars.

At this point, each of the Carols have taken the first step off the pinnacle of the pyramid down either side of their justification of their choice. Carol 1 is now on the first step down from the top on the left hand side that her actions were justified. Carol 2 is on the first step down on the right hand side, justifying her choice of not stealing from work and doing the right thing.

At the end of the working day, Carol number 1 has compiled a mental list to justify what she did and feels she deserved the money, and nobody was hurt, so there's no reason why she shouldn't have done it. Meanwhile, Carol number 2 has thought back to all of the times the company had been good to her in the past, and whatever the reason for their decision, she was glad to have had any bonus at all and grateful for a good job with a wonderful company. Each of the Carols have now taken further steps down either side of the pyramid.

Now something interesting happens. Their beliefs are about to undergo changes. This belief change will happen to both Carols, as number 1 has thoughts on theft that are now about to be realigned. She changes her opinion on theft and now dismisses it as being something that's not that bad. No physical harm has come to anyone, and it's a victimless crime. Whereas Carol 2 is down the opposite side of the pyramid; her belief that theft is wrong has now been reinforced, with events that unfold around both of the Carols confirming their choice was the right one. Maybe someone gets fired for stealing, and Carol 2 believes they deserve all they get as it's so wrong and is glad she never did anything so heinous when she'd had multiple opportunities to do so. Possibly even blocking out the fact that the thought had ever even crossed her mind, because, let's face it, Carol number 2 does not agree with theft in any way. Conversely,

Carol 1 is enjoying debts that are paid off due to her investing some of her ill-gotten gains, which in her mind is position she wouldn't have been in, if she hadn't taken the money she took on that fateful day.

As more time goes by, the pair of Carols that exist in parallel lives have two completely different beliefs when it comes to stealing. One believes it's not a big deal, and the other believes it's an awful crime. This demonstrates how one decision can alter the entire path of your life and completely change your beliefs.Moreover psychology has proven that if a person has gotten away with something once, they're more likely to do it again. This can lead to how a seemingly good person can end up being the kind of person that steals money from work, time and time again, usually increasing the amount taken each time, and not feel like they're doing something they shouldn't. I bring this up to help you to understand the self-justification pyramid system, and how a person can end up in a completely different place with just one small decision being the catalyst. This section is going to be extremely pertinent later on when we cover the method of extracting confessions. It is important you understand that a person accused of embezzling thousands of dollars from the company they work for didn't just get up one morning and decide to steal money from work. I've never come across a case yet where someone has said to themselves, "I fancy a career change; I think I'll become a thief." Events like this come about through a minor decision that has snowballed. All the time being justified in the mind of the person doing it. You will see how relevant and how powerful this information is when we go into the methods of extracting a confession, but there are a few other areas to cover first.

13. The Most Important Question to ask When a Person's Telling All

An admission is not necessarily a full confession! There might be an instance where a person is caught in the act of doing something and confesses to the one thing they were caught doing, but not to the full list of things they were in the process of doing.

So, when you ask a person what they were doing at the time they were caught and they start confessing, the single most important question you need to ask is, "What else?"

I'm going to use a story of a friend of mine as an example (some details may have been changed).

A prisoner of war was captured by the US military and was being questioned.

INT = Interrogator **POW** = Prisoner of War

INT: What were you doing at the time of being captured?

POW: Planting IEDs

INT: What else?

POW: Reconnaissance

INT: What else?

POW: Recording videos

INT: What else?

POW: Hiding weapons.

INT: What else?

POW: That was it.

INT: Are you sure?

POW: Yes, that was everything.

In most instances, the interrogator would have asked the question and have been satisfied with the first answer, happy with a confession, then moved on and not got any more information from the detainee.

By asking "what else", the detainee was under the impression that the interrogator had more information than he actually did. Of course, he can go back and revisit any of the specific areas again later on, but now he has several to choose from and not just one.

For the record, in the example above the detainee actually told the interrogator at the end of the session that he genuinely believed that he knew everything about him simply because he kept asking "what else". To the point that when the interrogator asked, "Are you sure?", he had to think very hard in case there was anything he'd missed that the interrogator knew that the detainee hadn't remembered. The belief alone that the interrogator knew everything was enough to get a full confession from the detainee. Proving that the words "what else" can be extremely powerful indeed.

Equally as effective, if not even more so, is the power of silence. Psychology has proved that people feel exceptionally awkward in the event of uncomfortable silence. This causes them to want to fill the gap. They feel the need to end the awkward silence by filling the void with anything they can. They will speak, even if at first they just repeat what they've said in a slightly different way. Once again, remain silent. They *will* continue.

One of the reasons this method of remaining silent is so powerful is that it creates so many questions in the mind of the other person. "Do they believe me? Do they know something I don't? Why haven't they said anything? Are they waiting for me to say more?" As they are internally asking themselves all these questions their thoughts run away with them, and they begin to panic, and people don't make good decisions when they're in a state of panic. They will start to spew out all sorts of verbal diarrhea in order to fill that awkward silence.

This tactic can be used in many circumstances. I have even used it to negotiate the price when buying a car. It can take some practice and, when learning, can even make you feel as uncomfortable as the person you're using it on. Just remember to treat it like a game; whoever speaks first, loses!

This is when you're going to want to unleash your competitive side and work as hard as you can to win by staying silent. Like with many other skills, the more you do it the easier you will find it, but I imagine for most people they will find it very uncomfortable at first. Just remember, if you're finding it uncomfortable, imagine how uncomfortable they're finding it. To help you, try counting in your head each time you use this technique, you can see if you can set new records. By doing this it will help occupy your mind as you wait without feeling as awkward as you could. The whole thing will seem longer than it actually is if your mind is not being occupied with another task.

14. Emotions - A Lesson of the Relevance of the Emotional Link

In the event of an odious crime, a guilty person will tend to distance themselves emotionally from the events. For example, if an innocent person were accused of rape, they would have no problem in saying something like, "I didn't rape her", whereas a guilty person might try to avoid using the word rape and replace it with something else, saying something like "I did not assault her".

Other ways emotional distancing can take place would be in cases like theft, where they might replace the word "stole" with "took", or something very similar. These are very basic cases of how emotional distancing can happen, but they can be more complex. Now that you have an idea of what it means we can look into it further.

We did cover this from a slightly different angle earlier in the book when we explored methods of revealing guilt. As we established, you can reveal guilt in the event of a false accusation by simply asking, "How did that make you feel?" and listening carefully to the response. If they respond with something along the lines of "hurt", "sad", "angry", or "scared", then you can consider this a normal response. If, however, they respond with a shrug and answer with something like, "I don't know. Sad, I guess." Then you can consider this a possible sign of guilt. If someone is being honest they shouldn't need to guess how they feel. They don't need to think about it. They just recall the memory of how they were feeling. When people are lying, however, they tend to have to create an emotion that they feel fits the scenario. Look for a delay in the answer or any signs that the person needs to think about it.

There is a subject I feel needs to be addressed here which may not seem relevant at first, but the reasons for its inclusion will hopefully become apparent as we look into it, and that is the subject of NPD, or Narcissistic Personality Disorder. The primary reason for raising this point is the key fact attached to the disorder itself. NPD is due to an underdeveloped part of the brain responsible for empathy. With that in mind, it can be difficult to look for emotive reactions and facial expressions that would assist you in your ability to read a person.

The word 'narcissist' comes from Greek mythology in which a young and very handsome hunter named Narcissus stops after a long and exhausting morning of hunting to drink water from the crystal-clear waters of the spring. However, when he lies down at the pool's edge and looks down to see his reflection in the water's surface, he falls in love with his own beauty. He refuses to drink the water for fear of disrupting the beautiful image and instead lies staring at his own reflection, unable to pull himself away. He lay at the side of the pool infatuated with his own looks until he died; a flower (Narcissus) marks the place where he met his demise. The Narcissus flower looks very much like a daffodil but has white petals around the yellow center instead of being yellow all over. Now that you have had a little history lesson on the origins of the name, let's explore the disorder itself a little more.

A 30-year study conducted in the 1980s found around 30% of people can display narcissistic traits, whereas 70% show empathy. 30 years later, however, the same study shows that since the arrival of the much picked upon millennial generation with its increased use of technology, specifically social media, along with many other lifestyle changes for the vast majority of people, the inverse of those numbers is now the case. Only 30% show empathy, and 70% display narcissistic tendencies. Whether there's any correlation between the use of social media and this statistical inversion, or if it's solely due to other societal changes, I don't know. Maybe one day another study might tell us more. Interestingly, though, I have recently been told that there is a direct correlation between males on social media using filters (such as the dog filter on Snapchat) and narcissism. The data seems to show that if the user has a filter (even more so if it's a Snapchat dog filter) in his profile picture, then there's a pretty high chance that he's a narcissist. This isn't to say that this is the case every time, but it appears to be the case in a high percentage of subjects. This is only the case with males though, for some reason. Let's explore the subject a little further.

Not every narcissist has Narcissistic Personality Disorder (NPD), as narcissism is a spectrum. People who are at the highest end of the spectrum are those that are classified as having NPD, but others, still with narcissistic traits, may fall on the lower end of the narcissistic spectrum.

So narcissism itself has four primary categories as it were, which are overt, covert, communal, and malignant (or antagonistic).

The overt narcissist can usually be easily identified because they tend to be loud, arrogant, insensitive to the needs of others, and always thirsty for compliments. Their behaviors can be easily observed by others and tend to show up as 'big' in a room.

A covert narcissist is someone who craves admiration and importance, as well as lacking empathy toward others, but can act in a different way than an overt narcissist. When considering the behaviors of narcissists, it might be hard to imagine how someone could be a narcissist and be inhibited in their approach and behavior.

A communal narcissist would be a person who grandiosely views himself as 'the most helpful person he knows,' or 'the most caring person in his social surroundings,' and 'extraordinarily trustworthy'.

In the popular conception, malignant narcissism is a form of narcissistic personality disorder that is highly abusive. People with this personality supposedly get a sense of satisfaction from hurting others and may frequently manipulate people or lie to gain money, acclaim, and other things they desire. The malignant narcissist is the most dangerous of all.

With this in mind, I feel it's important to address another aspect here too, which is that having narcissistic traits does not make a person a narcissist. I compare this to someone with a temper, they don't go around smashing things up and growling angrily to everyone all the time. Narcissism is a trait just like any other, and just like temper, can come and go. Keep this in mind when 'labelling' someone as a narcissist, are they actually a narcissist? Or do they just have narcissistic traits?

Also, keep in mind that we all have narcissistic traits to some degree. If we didn't then we would never ask for the promotion or raise we feel we deserve, we would never ask that person we like on a date, to a certain degree, a healthy level of a narcissism is needed, as long as the part of the brain that regulates it kicks in and stops you from becoming an un-empathetic person who cares about nobody other than themselves.

Identifying a narcissist can be reasonably easy according to a 2014 study at Ohio University. It can be as simple as asking one question, which is simply, "are you a narcissist?". Believe it or not, it's proved to be almost equally as effective as a clinical test for NPD, yielding almost identical results. The reason for this is that a person who is aware they are a narcissist doesn't view their traits, or even the fact that they are a narcissist, in a negative way. Therefore, they don't feel the need to hide the fact and will usually quite happily admit to it. Of course, this isn't a 100% foolproof system, but it can be quite revealing.

There are other ways you can identify a narcissist with some of the following questions.

1) What are your biggest hurts? – A narcissist wouldn't understand this question, or they may see it as stupid. They believe themselves to be above all that 'feelings' stuff and would view it as a weakness.

2) What ways do you need to grow/change? – A narcissist would already see themselves as perfect, so to suggest they need to change also suggests they are not. They would be offended by the thought of it and would react accordingly. If they do

remain calm and give an answer, then listen to what is being said. Are they referring to aspects of self-improvement when they answer? Or are they telling you about superficial changes they feel they might want. Such as their car, house, or job etc.

3) Why do you love me? – Listen carefully to how they answer. Are they listing traits and qualities or are they listing goods and services that you provide for them? For example, do they answer with things like similar interests and feelings or are they telling you about all the things you do for them?

Of course, these questions are only a way to help you determine the possibility of whether someone is a narcissist or not and are not meant as a replacement for an actual clinical test. They are definitely not meant to be considered as a means of confirming with definitive accuracy if a person is a narcissist or not.

The reason I've covered the topic of narcissism is because of the relevance to the emotional link. It is extremely hard to look for empathy in a person who has none. Keep this in mind when looking for deception and, as always, get a baseline for the person first. This includes their displays of feelings and emotions. This will help you when it comes to looking for the emotional links we've discussed above. They be missing purely because of the person and not necessarily because of deceit.

Assuming that so far you've managed to do everything right and implemented everything you've learned thus far, we're going to continue with how you would then work towards getting a confession in the next section.

15. Priming the Subject

In this section, we need to explore several lessons in psychology in order to gain a piece of the jigsaw that we will put together at the end to complete the picture. There are several layers to each area that we need to establish and then, when each part of the process comes together, you will see how it works to prime the subject ready to get them to confess. Some of the areas we are going to look into may not at first seem like they are relevant but go with it, and it will all make sense at the end.

As we have established, people's memories are pliable. So, in fact, are their thoughts and beliefs. Experiments in psychology have shown this phenomenon with the method of asking people who are single how happy they are. The same question asked but preceded by a question of how their dating life was going resulted in the participants reporting to be less happy than when not asked the preceding question. An experiment conducted at Warwick University in England implanted false memories subjects of them being in a hot air balloon ride as a child. In another psychology experiment, participants were asked to watch a video of a robbery. Later on, when asked to recall details of the robbery, the participants' responses could be influenced by the person simply asking the questions and making certain gestures. For example, if they pointed to their fingers while asking what jewellery was stolen, the participants stated that they saw rings being stolen. Pointing to the left wrist or a wristwatch elicited the response that they saw mostly watches being stolen, and the right wrist or a bracelet would result in them saying they mostly saw bracelets being stolen. So there you have it; sometimes you don't even have to speak to influence the thoughts of a person. This demonstrates exactly how easy it is to use these psychological tactics to steer a person into believing what you want them to believe.

Now imagine a suspect has been arrested and is in the interview room waiting to be questioned. The interviewer walks in and places a thick evidence folder on the table between them. The psychological impact that action alone has is enormous. How do I know? Because I've done it and seen it done. More to the point, the folder I used had very little in the way of anything in it. I had stuffed it with misprint pages and old note paper, along with a few other things, plus the single and only piece of evidence that I actually had.

I used the tactic of appearing to have overwhelming amounts of evidence. I asked about several events, all the time giving the impression I was certain of what happened and had evidence to support it. I then questioned the subject on the only event for which I had any evidence, appearing to be a little uncertain. When he failed to answer directly, I lifted the evidence folder, thumbed through it until I found the only piece of real evidence in there, and slipped it out. This give the impression everything I had said earlier was backed up with evidence and further reinforced the suspects belief, because if the one area I wasn't one hundred percent sure of, yet had evidence to back up the claims, then surely I also had evidence to substantiate the other areas that I was so certain of, right? Wrong; I had bluffed, but the suspect didn't know that.

All he knew (or at least all he thought he knew) was that I had masses of evidence against him and was just going through the formalities. He believed he had no other alternative than to tell me his version of events and be as truthful as he could be. So I sat there as he told me everything. His mind did the work for me. All I had was a single photograph, but he didn't know that. Using this tactic and the methods we're going to explore as we continue, a confession is pretty much inevitable.

Think of priming the subject a little like holding the door open for someone to exit a room and telling them that all the other doors out of the room are locked. You might rattle the handles of one or two that you know for sure are locked to reinforce what you are saying, but whether the rest of them are unlocked or not, the subject must believe that they are, and the only way out is by walking through the door that you're holding open for them. By the end of the whole process, the subject must have no thoughts that would remotely suggest there were other options and be grateful to you for holding the door open for them and showing them the only way out.

So priming the subject is all about showing them the door you want them to go through. They must walk through it, willingly and happily in the belief that there is no other option, and if you've done your job properly, they will be completely convinced that the door you're holding open for them is the only way for them to leave the room and move on with their life.

The most important aspect here is that they believe it was still their choice; that they had the freedom to choose whether to confess or not and decided of their own free will that it was the best option, even if it was their only one.

As it happens, the evidence folder is not the only method of priming the subject. Photos being passed to the interviewer during the middle of the interview; a detective coming in and whispering something to the interviewer in the middle of the interview, even a phone call where you give the impression that their associate or someone else is giving loads of information. These are all methods of giving the person the impression that they're in a position which is not going to be easy to get out of. Being on the phone and saying the words, "well, keep him talking while I speak to this one" can be an effective priming device. Glaring at the suspect can be enough to make them believe that they better get their side in quickly before someone else's story gets told first. There are many imaginative ways to prime the subject but I'm sure you get the idea.

It is occasionally advisable to start the interview process by sharing the evidence with the suspect in an attempt to get them to realize it's enough for a conviction, but at other times, it is advised to save all the evidence you have until after you've heard their story and then call them out on it, with the evidence forcing them to admit to a lie. If you do a really good job, however, you shouldn't need any of the evidence at all, your words, combined with the impression of evidence (whether you actually have it or not), will be enough to get the person to tell you everything.

A Gentle Push

Sometimes, in order to give the impression you know more than you do, you have to give the impression that there's more going on behind the scenes. For example: imagine the interview has been in progress for a minute or two, when another detective knocks at the door. The reason for the intrusion is to ask the interviewing detective a question.

Det1: Sorry for the intrusion, I just need to know where the suspect was between 7 and 8.

Det2: (knowing the suspect was on Fifth Avenue between 7 and 8) Hang on. (Flicks through the overstuffed evidence folder and walks over to the door) 4 'til 5, 6 'til 7 (quietly). Ah yes (a bit louder), 7 'til 8. Here it is, he was on Fifth Avenue.

Det1: Thanks (leaves the room).

This serves two purposes. Firstly, it gives the impression that the detective knows where the suspect's been all day and has had him under surveillance for a long period. So it gives the impression that if that one snippet of information in the entire folder is accurate, then all the other information in the rest of the folder must be accurate too.

Now imagine the detective goes on with the interview for a few more minutes and the detective comes knocking again. He opens the door and stands in the doorway with another question.

Det1: Sorry for intruding again, I need to know the evidence numbers of the files you have placing the suspect at the scene, how many fingerprints of his were lifted, DNA evidence, the CCTV camera footage reference number, and the witness details.

Det2: (giving an exasperated exhale as he stands up) Hang on a minute, I'll come out and give it to you." (Grabbing the thick evidence folder off the desk to step outside the interview room for a minute.)

Now the detective might not have any of that evidence, but the suspect thinks he does. That's the most important part. They have been given the impression that the odds are against them, and that overwhelming amounts of proof show that they did it. Even if they're not sure that you do actually have the evidence you say you do, you have planted the seed of doubt. That tiny seed, if watered, can be enough to get you what you want. Used either alone or in conjunction with other psychological tactics, this is a very powerful method of priming the subject.

The creation of severity – To help you get to grips with how effective the technique of priming a person is, I want you to imagine the following scenario:

You come home from work and your spouse asks you, "Did you use my laptop today?"

Now Image the same scenario but before that question, your spouse says, "I want to ask you a question but before you answer, think very carefully about what you're going to say and what your response is. Now, don't just answer, take the time to think carefully, did you use my laptop today?"

Can you see how by priming the subject I've raised the potential severity level of the question? This single tactic has now taken what might normally be dismissed as a very casual question and turned it into something that has the person questioning how much trouble they could be in, as well as having planted the seed that there's more going on than your spouse just wanting to know if you've used their laptop. This becomes exceptionally more powerful when a person is guilty of a crime and facing severe consequences.

At this point, we're going to go deeper into the psychology of lying and how to dissect the lie in order to get to the truth. Earlier, when we discussed the two primary reasons people lie, we will now see how this will come into play with priming the subject to get a confession.

First, we need to take a quick look beyond the two primary reasons people lie and step back to view the bigger picture. Lying may allow the subject to feel a perceived level of control over a situation by manipulating it to their favor. It can also be a form of defense mechanism that (seemingly to them) prevents them from being or feeling vulnerability or discomfort, by not opening up and revealing their true self. The aim is to minimize the chances of being rejected, criticized, or feeling disappointed in them. Needless to say, for a deeply insecure person, the very thought of this can be unbearable. When someone is lying and they are rejected, there's a rational sense of there being a reason for the rejection. On the flipside, when a person who is being open and honest is rejected, this might feel to them as though they're fundamentally disliked, which can have a seriously negative effect on their self-esteem.

On occasions, people repeat what has previously worked for them. Lying in order to create an alternative persona might be an unconscious behavior that gets repeated as a result of past experiences. In other words, that person hasn't learnt how to relate to others effectively. For example; it's possible that they may have faced difficulties in their upbringing such as violent parents, so they had to create a world of their own (often lying to themselves or developing a habit of lying to others). It's not uncommon. People change their personality somewhat and have an alter ego of sorts. After a long time living in this role, the new way of living becomes who they are.

As a potential extension of the defense mechanism I mentioned earlier, people may also occasionally lie to avoid difficult situations and try to hide the feelings that come with them, feelings like depression, sadness, guilt, and anxiety. Low self-esteem can make it harder to cope with these feelings. Lying can enable a person to and avoid situations where they may have to confront these overwhelming feelings in the short-term. It is, however, important to be aware that suppressing your thoughts and feelings into your subconscious is not a solution, and they can and will affect you in the long term, this is unavoidable and is the basis of psychoanalytic therapy.

Another common reason people lie, is a fear of hurting or letting a person down. Some people find it extremely difficult to deal with the feelings that come with disappointing another person. In this case, you have to ask yourself, who is being protected here? The person being lied to, or the person telling the lie. As I mentioned before, the two primary reasons for lying are protection and gain, so what is at the root of lying to a person to avoid hurting their feelings? Is it protection for them? Or is protection for the person telling the lie in order to avoid their own feelings that arise when hurting or disappointing someone? In most cases, it's the latter. People don't want that negative feeling associated with making another person feel bad. The very thought of disappointing someone or letting them down is overwhelmingly awful for them, so the temporary discomfort of lying in the present moment to avoid any ill feeling outweighs the negative ill feeling they get by telling a lie. It could be argued that this is both for protection and gain, but not for the person being lied to but the person telling the lie. You could be under the impression that this is a selfish reason because it centers on protecting them from taking responsibility for the disappointment; most of the time, the person being lied to usually wants to know the truth, whatever it is.

From the opposing point of view, when the other person senses that they're being lied to, no matter how big or small the lie (or the reasons behind it) it can affect their ability to trust the person who has lied to them in more ways than one. Should they see through the lies, even if it's observed and identified as insecurity or a lack of confidence, this can affect their respect and overall judgement of the person.

The majority of the time, people are more accepting of others' flaws and imperfections when that person is open and transparent about them. In other words, they own their imperfections. Often, this is in fact very endearing to us as humans (if you want to know more about the psychology behind this, research 'The Pratfall Effect'). It's also liberating and can act as a massive release for us as individuals when we openly acknowledge and come clean about our weaknesses and mistakes, something that many people find extremely difficult to do. The act of acknowledgement alone can sometimes be the hardest part, and can occasionally require some form of professional coercion to be brought to the surface and made visible for the subject.

The reason I have brought these factors to your attention is as follows: For you to identify if a lie is for protection or gain is the first hurdle, but sometimes you have to ask who is actually the one being protected. You may feel like it's the person who might be on the receiving end of unpleasant news or disappointment, but as I mentioned, it's actually not. So the first thing to address is to make sure you have identified the right person who will be protected or will gain by the lie being told. Secondly, you need to address the fact we established afterwards, which is; sometimes it can be subconscious or difficult for the subject to admit, especially if it means they have to acknowledge their flaws and imperfections. So you will have to take this into account when trying to get to the truth. Can you somehow ascertain the truth without causing a conflict of emotions within the subject? Can you get them to confess to a lie, while still maintaining their denial of any personal issues they may have with themselves?

With careful planning and keeping the end result in mind you can pre-empt a rough script of how the conversation will more than likely go. Thus, you can structure the framework of the conversation to lead to where you want it to go. I have taught elicitation skills to people and how to steer a conversation, and some of these skills may be useful here. If you want to know more about elicitation and how to control a conversation, then please check out my website (gavinstoneauthor.com). For the moment, though, all you have to do is put yourself in the other person's shoes. Attempt to see things their way and understand the reason behind their deception. With this in mind, you might be able to figure out if there are other factors that they may possibly want to keep concealed in order to save face. It's down to you to offer them an "out" which will allow them to do this and ultimately still get to the truth. The last thing you want is to expose someone's hidden fears in order to get to a truth that is not anywhere near as uncomfortable for them as their fears may be. You have to find a way to allow them to keep their hidden secrets concealed while still being open and honest about the event you want information on.

I have a friend who was a prison psychologist and regularly helped offenders with particular issues. Sometimes she would sit with a group of offenders in a room in one sitting, and other times she'd see them on an individual basis. She told me how a person's account of an event can change dramatically when they're with their peers, compared to when she sees the individual on a one-to-one basis. She can, however, from this mixed dynamic form enough information to address issues with the offender without 'calling them out'. Essentially, she can get to the truth without causing them undue embarrassment.

I'm letting you know about this because sometimes people can be so hell-bent on getting the truth that they focus on that alone and can't figure out the reasons they keep getting blocked when they know the subject is lying and are doing what they think is right to expose the lie, not realizing that exposing the lie might also inadvertently expose other aspects of the individual's life that they'd rather were kept secret. Sometimes, you have to step back and look at the bigger picture.

Occasionally, you can't pinpoint the exact reason a person is trying to keep something concealed, so you either have to speculate on possibilities, or go for the second option (that many people find difficult), which is to accept that there is a reason the subject might not want the truth to be known, and you will never know what it is. If you can't work it out, sometimes you just have to operate on that conclusion and accept that you're not going to find out. A very hard task for many, as the inherent human need for closure is so exceptionally..

You see.

To help reinforce this point I'm going to teach you a little psychology trick. If you want to get a song stuck in someone's head, you simply sing half of the main line from the chorus or if it has a particularly strong intro, then half of the first line of the song. As an example I was going to use the song Carly Simon wrote about me but decided a well-known globally recognized song by all age groups, was more suitable. So let's put it to the test, sing along with me:

"In the jungle, the mighty jungle, the….."

And stop.

Whether you like it or not, your brain really wants to sing "Lion sleeps tonight." and even if you fight it, you're aware of the desire to continue. Moreover, if you were to sing this half line at a low volume around your other half or work colleagues, then you are almost guaranteed to hear them singing it around the house or office for the rest of the day. It works, I've tried it. If you want some real fun, see if you can get an entire department singing a rendition of 'In the jungle' while you're working on your spreadsheets.

The only caveat with this of course, is that the person you're attempting this on must know the song. If they don't then the whole thing has been a waste of time. So pick a popular tune when you decide to test it.

Have a little fun and now you know the power of the human need for closure.

If you can bring yourself to function on the concept of not knowing, yet continue to operate, then you can concentrate on getting to the truth, without being distracted by the details you **want** but don't necessarily **need** to know. Sometimes, knowing a person did something is enough, and you don't always need to know why.

I've added this little part as a reminder to you to stay focused on what your aim is when it comes to getting to the truth. I don't want you to stray from your predetermined path with distractions about finding out the "why" when your goal was to confirm the "if". There are so many ways in which you can be distracted. I did contemplate putting them in here, but the last thing I want is to bore you with a list. The main concept is simply to remember to stay on track, practice, and make a mental note of any time you digress and do whatever it takes to reset and concentrate on reaching your goal. Your goal being not getting side-tracked and ascertaining the truth.

Liars can very easily manipulate a situation and before you know it, you're going around in verbal circles on a topic that has nothing to do with the one you set out to get to. Using the strategy of constantly stopping, assessing and seeing if what you're doing is going to get you any closer to the truth, or further away, will guide you and help you to stay on track. And if you're worried about whether the subject will willingly talk or not, read the next section, and all will be revealed.

16. The Right to Remain Silent

D ifferent studies from around the world show a variety of suspects that waive their Miranda rights the majority of the time. The numbers from each country and study may vary but not greatly. In fact, a recent study showed that people who invoke the right to remain silent are as few as only 5 percent! While this number is from only one study in one country, others show the people willing to waive their Miranda rights can be anything from 80 to 95 percent of the time. With that in mind, it shows us exactly how much people are willing to talk and not keep their mouths shut, even if it could get them into trouble.

Police Methods of Extracting a confession

In the UK, the vast majority of the entire policing system relies heavily on confessions. People's desire to talk (especially about themselves) is usually enough for the police to get what they need. Over the years, it's been established by police, military, and intelligence agencies worldwide that if you torture a man, he will tell you anything. Which is a problem within itself. Cause a man enough pain and he will say whatever it takes to make the pain stop, even if it's not true. This is the problem faced by most of the government organizations.

So how do you get a man to confess to committing a crime? Well, to explain this we need to look into the reasons he has for lying for a short while. Earlier on we talked about the only two reasons a person lies, protection or gain. In an instance where a person is talking to the police it would fall into the protection category. This will now take us down the road of psychology for a moment, but you have to ask yourself, does he want to move towards or away from something? I imagine his direction would be away, away from the potential incarceration. Now you know he wishes to avoid the ramifications of the situation, you are closer to finding his motivation to lie. At this point, you have to move carefully to lessen the perceived severity of the situation and increase the desire to be truthful. We will go into that more deeply later on when we look at getting a person to confess to everything, but for now, we will continue with a person's deep need to talk.

As we've established, it's the fear of possible repercussions that makes a person want to tell a lie in the first place. So usually when Britain's Metropolitan police have somebody in the interview room, they rely on a person's desire to talk and lack of desire to face penalization. So they do their best to keep an informal tone and frequently tend to begin the interview with an opening line like:

"Don't worry, you're not in any trouble, we just want to hear your side of the story."

This simple little line goes a long way in opening up the interview for the suspect to start telling their side. Most of the time, letting them just ramble on for long enough, with the occasional interjection to steer the course of the conversation, is sufficient to get the desired results.

If the person starts with an attitude of, "I've got nothing to say", a simple baiting process is the next step.

I'll create a scenario. Let's say Dave is in the interview room accused of assaulting John at a local bar. Dave is sitting and saying nothing even after the first attempt of coercing a confession has been applied.

It's worth mentioning here that most police officers will attempt to continue communicating, even after being told by the suspect that they wish to remain silent. Often the line, "that's fine, you don't have to talk, just listen." is enough to initiate the process. The officer relies heavily on the suspect getting wound up and jumping in to 'right the wrongs'. They may even dismiss altogether the fact that the suspect has requested to remain silent and carry on regardless. It is, after all, down to the suspect to control his own mouth and simply not talk. The police, however, know that's easier said than done.

The interviewing officer might say something like:

"Ok, I understand if you don't want to talk, that's fine. All we want to do is clear up the facts. So, as we understand, John was having a drink with his wife, and you came in shouting, went to hit John in the face, missed and hit his shoulder and John slapped you across the face knocking you clean out on to the floor."

This is almost teasing Dave to go into a rant, and the officers would expect a response along the lines of:

"No, it was him who was shouting at me, and I didn't miss, I hit him clean in the jaw, and he never even tried to hit me back!"

And there you have it. Confession.

Feeding False Information

Assuming Dave is a little smarter than the average suspect and still doesn't say anything, the officer might then continue with something like this:

(All the time remaining in a soft and friendly tone)

"Oh, John reckons you hit his wife too. You're not a woman-beater, are you?"

The conversation might then go a little like this:

D) No! I never touched his wife!

I.O.) Look, it's ok, I understand it might have been by accident. I get how these things happen. You take a swing for John and accidently smack his wife in the face. It's not your fault.

D) No, I didn't touch her at all.

I.O.) Ok, so you get into a brawl and during the ruckus she gets knocked. It's understandable, she was right there next to where you were fighting.

D) No, she wasn't, she was at the back of the room and we were fighting next to the bar. She was nowhere near us when we were fighting!

Yet again, another confession.

As I said earlier, people love to talk, especially if it's about themselves and even more so if there's any sense of injustice in what a person is saying. In the conversation above, the interviewing officer was utilizing his skills to play on Dave's pride and ego in order to get him to confess. Towards the end, simply by distorting the facts to demonstrate a minor injustice (being falsely accused of hitting John's wife), the interviewing officer was able to extract a confession. Dave's deep need to prevent injustice was so strong that it outweighed the want to remain un-convicted for his assault against John.

This technique is the primary basis for the British police and many other law enforcement agencies all over the world. A lot of police forces have come to realize that it's a lot more effective than the old 'good cop, bad cop' routine. Don't get me wrong, some good old fashioned police work has to be done a lot of the time, it's not as simple as just getting a person into a room and winding them up. You will need to have statements and evidence of some description to have a suspect in the room in the first place. This book is about deception detection, though, and not how to conduct an investigation. So, let's get back to the subject we're on.

This method can also be used in other situations. Instead of just verbally making false accusations, the interviewing officer might, for example, show a knife as a murder weapon. The suspect might not react, so they show him a shirt with blood on it. Again, the suspect might not react, but then they show him a wristwatch with blood splatter on the face. The suspect, not recognizing the watch, might blurt out:

"That's not mine."

This confirms the interviewing officer's thoughts. Denial of ownership of a watch they knew wasn't his is the flipside of the coin and acts as confirmation that the other two items shown *did* belong to the suspect.

Divide and Conquer

Another method used by the police is simply to play friends or colleagues off against each other. They put them into two separate interview rooms and tell each of them that their mate is in the other room confessing to everything.

To take things a little further, an interviewing officer might use a technique that makes the conversation go something like this:

I.O.) So, Ryan, your mate Stewart's in the other room saying it was all your idea, looks like he's the innocent party in all of this, led astray by you.

R) It wasn't my idea! Stewart was the one who thought of it all, he wanted to rob the place, not me.

And you have your confession.

On a related note here: liars in pairs tend not to engage as much as truth-tellers who will bat the conversation back and forth. That's a little tip for when you don't have the advantage of splitting two people up which will give you the advantage to spot deception when used with the other methods in this book.

Chain of Events

Another method used is simply to get a person to run through the chain of events, making notes of the times and details, then in order to check for consistency, they request the suspect to run through the chain of events backwards. This can really throw the suspect off guard and cause them to get mixed up in cases of deceit. In the event of two people being interviewed and the stories matching, the interviewing officer might throw in a false statement allegedly made by the other suspect to see the result. For example he might make out that the second suspect stopped at a fast food establishment at some point in his story. Making the conversation go a little like this:

I.O.) So you left the bar at eleven that night and went home with Stewart?"

R) Yes, I've told you this already.

I.O.) So what time did you stop to get Little Caesars?

R) What?

I.O.) Well Stewart said you stopped for gas on the way home and grabbed a Little Caesars to eat on the way back

R) Oh yeah, that was about half-eleven I think.

The interviewing officer will then use the same tactic on Stewart only this time he might say they stopped at KFC. Stewart confirms his friend's story and result. The stories don't match. Now the interviewing officer has a mass of ammunition to use, and in the event of not being able to get a confession then and there, the inconsistencies will come out in a court of law, highlighting the duo's guilt and deceit.

There are other tactics and techniques used by the police, but at least I've highlighted a handful of the main ones for you. So how does this help you? Well, as you can see, we've covered a lot about playing to pride and ego, which is a major factor when it comes to confessions for law enforcement agencies, but let's consider a different angle completely.

Drawing conclusions

A method used by some law enforcement agencies is to get a suspect to draw a diagram to act as a visual aid to their statement. This simple method of obtaining a visual representation of an event can act as a key element in detecting deception. A person lying about a scenario will usually draw the situation from above. A plan-like drawing, looking down on the whole scene. This is a subconscious attempt of detachment from the lie. A way of separating themselves from the deceit. If the person is being truthful, they will draw everything from ground level with themselves amongst the people of the event in question. They illustrate themselves as a part of the whole thing, usually from the point of view of their own eyes and including other people. If a person is lying, they will frequently leave other people out of the diagram unless they are a part of the drawn explanation.

Raising the Bar

Questioning someone you know is one thing but what about questioning complete strangers?

Well, I have a little something for you to use there too. A strategy used by a UK based security organization when questioning commuters at an airport prior to flight have developed a simple trick. A tactical questioning method that works by getting the individual to commit to openness first.

Set up in a way that appears to be more of an informal chat than an interrogation, the interviewer simply begins by asking:

"How honest a person do you consider yourself to be?"

Now nobody likes to be considered dishonest, so they tend to convey how much of an honest and integral person they are. Once they have spent a set amount of time attempting to convince you of their complete honesty, they are almost committed to being transparent. It may seem a little unlikely but the person then tends to go out of their way to prove their statement of how honest they are. A little like what I mentioned earlier about playing to someone's ego. If you inflate their ego enough and fill them with self-pride when it comes to being co-operative, you'd be surprised how far it will get you.

Of course once you've asked the question, they themselves have raised the bar and the right form of tactical questioning can get you the answers you need. Now when I say tactical questioning, I mean asking pre-planned open ended questions in a specific order, not the type of tactical questioning some unscrupulous military establishments perform with pain compliance tools.

In the past I have had to go through being interviewed around the head with a phone book and I can assure you it wasn't pleasant.

Another occasion a couple of guys interviewed the shit out of me for over two hours because I wouldn't answer a specific question the way they liked. Which obviously reinforces what I said previously about physical interrogation not always being the best method. A person is able to take a certain amount of pain but when they reach the threshold they will simply tell you anything you want to hear to get you to stop inflicting the pain upon them, whether it's true or not.

Even some of the world's most infamous organizations from the Middle East have realized that the fear of pain can be more intimidating than the pain itself. The recent realization is that there is no better weapon inside a man's mind than the thoughts he creates himself. Whether this is through fear of physical pain or like in the previous instances, fear of being caught out in a lie. Allowing a person's mind to work overtime on the feelings of guilt and fear, will create a desire to alleviate those feelings by attempting some sort of explanation. This is the point where you have the advantage, and using the system I'll show you later on, will allow you to utilize it to lever it in your favor in huge way.

17. Extracting a Confession

Having spent years not only using elicitation techniques but also training and teaching them to other people too, I need to stress the importance of this section. Rapport-building and elicitation are highly effective; however, they **must** be used from the beginning of your confession extraction. The reason for this is simple. If you start off your inquiry in a certain manner, and your questions set the tone for an interview, then attempting to transition to rapport-building halfway through will stand out like a sore thumb. The subject will pick up on the change, becoming aware of a shift and will automatically become suspicious. This will put them on guard, even if it's only subconsciously. Their defenses will go up as opposed to down, preventing you from achieving the desired effect you would normally have when implementing these techniques.

Elicitation is an extremely powerful tool, so much so that I have stated on multiple occasions that elicitation is probably the single most important skill a spy can possess. In fact, no matter how good a recruit is at all of the other skills, if they don't have the ability to utilize elicitation then there's no point in them carrying on. After all, we're in the trade of obtaining secrets. It's no good knowing how to shoot or be proficient in escape and evasion if you're not able to get the information you need to escape with.

So what exactly is elicitation and how does it work? Put simply, elicitation is the act of obtaining information from a person in an unassuming manner, by use of provocative statements as opposed to questions. Questions naturally put people on guard. You create a tennis match of question and answer, which bounces back and forth between you and the person you're trying to get the information from. This automatically has a person in a defensive mode. The feeling of being interrogated is far from pleasant; a conversation on the other hand doesn't have that same interview style feeling attached to it. A conversation is pleasant and consists of the two-way sharing of thoughts, opinions, and experiences etc.

A quick example of the use of elicitation techniques in the form of a provocative statement as opposed to a question is as follows:

Instead of asking your Uber driver: "Do you ever have any customers doing weird things in your car?"

You make the statement: "I bet you've got some crazy stories to tell about the weird things you've seen and heard from customers in your car."

Because this is a statement and not a question, it doesn't get the person to react with concern. They don't ask themselves why you're asking them questions and therefore don't feel the need to be cautious with their answer. They see the whole event as just having a harmless conversation. I have personally obtained masses of information from people just by starting the sentence with the words "I bet…" Of course the type of elicitation I teach goes much deeper and is a lot more extensive, but this has given you an example of how using elicitation is so much more effective than just asking questions.

(Go to my website - gavinstone.us – for more information on the training I offer)

As I mentioned, however, you can't be halfway through an interview and suddenly switch to attempting elicitation techniques with the subject. They will sense something is off, so you need to set the tone from the beginning and start as you intend to continue, using elicitation as a tool and building rapport as you go. One of the best and most effective ways of building rapport rapidly is with the use of NLP and Social Engineering. I'm a certified NLP practitioner and can tell you how powerful it can be first hand when used correctly. As with anything in life, what you learn and where you learn it from can have a dramatic impact on your perception of a subject. I mention this because there are people I have spoken to in the past who have done a $7 online NLP course that lasted 3 hours and awarded them a "print-it-yourself" certificate, then complained that NLP was a waste of time and doesn't work. Of course it doesn't work if you've paid $7 to learn it. Would you work for $7?

My advice is if you really want to learn NLP and want something of quality and value that will give you real achievable advantage, then learn it from a reputable NLP practitioner who is recommended and long established. It really can be a very useful tool, but like with most things, you get what you pay for.

NLP will give anyone a huge advantage when it comes to rapport-building techniques. It has many other beneficial areas too, but that's something you can explore if you feel the need. Teamed up with the elicitation techniques I use and the psychology aspects I implement, extracting a confession is almost a step-by-step walk through process. I'll do my best to give you a template for it in this section.

First off, realize that you are attempting to coerce information from someone who is, for whatever reason, not wanting to give you that information. So in order to elicit that information from them, you have to tread carefully. If you don't probe in the right way then you're not going to get what you want. At the same time, if you probe too vigorously then it stands a chance the person will go into a defensive mode and withhold the information too.

So how do you get the mix right? Well, it's a case of knowing the main elements of coercion and applying them simultaneously. One of the best examples of this is an area I spent some time studying a few years ago, when I was first learning to write.

It's called copywriting. Which is basically sales letters or emails and, in some instances, videos. When I first looked into copywriting, I was surprised at exactly how much money could be earned by simply writing a sales letter. You can earn a fixed fee or royalties for your work, sometimes both. But what is it? I hear you ask, well, the best way to describe it is persuasive writing. How often have you had junk mail through your door? I'm pretty certain you've had quite a lot of it. Well junk mail and sales emails are written in a very specific way. Now the latest step up from this seems to be links to sales videos. Again the script is written in a very specific way. It's laid out to make you a promise. Show you proof of the product working and how great it is. Tell you how you can't live without it. Demonstrate how much better it's made other people's lives. Finally wrapping up with a bonus or two and offering it to you at a discounted price if you buy now?

Sound familiar?

Well let's break it down. To start with the product is irrelevant; it's what's being said that's important.

- The promise is how your life will change with this product. That's where they get your sole attention or at least peak your interest.

- They show you proof that it is what they say it is, or does what it says it will. This eliminates any doubts you may have had at any point, extinguishing them before they've even had a chance to enter your thoughts sometimes.

- Then the testimonials. Extremely powerful tools. People are influenced by other people. How many times have you seen other people doing something and because it looks good, fun, or useful, and you wanted to have a go too?

- Then the unexpected bonus, which is just to sweeten the pot, and when you find out you can get it cheaper than you expected to, sometimes ends up being the final decider.

- The very last part is the time constraint, keeping you in a mode of thinking in the 'here and now', instead of thinking things like: "Will my life actually be better with this product?" or "Is it just going to be another piece of unused junk in the attic?"

Instead of these questions creeping into your head, the visual ticking of the clock in the corner of the screen to let you know how much time is left to make your purchase keeps you from letting these thoughts in and has you dialling 1-800-stitch-me-up with your card details.

It's that mode of short-term thinking that you have to ensure the person you're questioning remains in. The areas to cover for this are as below.

1. Isolation from external information sources

2. Acceptance of what is being delivered

3. Subservient thought pattern

4. Kept from long-term thought & ramifications

So let's break that system down even further.

Isolation from external information sources

In the sales video scenario, your attention is deliberately kept using a system called open loops. They promise to answer a question after a few minutes, but before giving you the answer to that question, they create another open loop. So in effect, when you get the answer you were after, you want to keep watching because you want the answer to the next open loop. And the cycle continues until they get to the pitch. This enables the sellers to keep your attention solely their video. That way, the only information source you have is coming from them. Isolating you and keeping you on the receiving end of a one-way flow of data. Of course, the only data you'll get is what they choose to give you.

Acceptance of what is being delivered

Once more you're going through the pattern of being brainwashed as "Derek from Ohio" is one of the many people who will be giving you his testimonial on how great his life is now he has this fantastic product. I don't even know what it is and I already want one!

The constant bombardment of people telling you how much better your life will be if you get one too reinforces the thoughts forming in your head and assists in justifying your about-to-be-made purchase. As I said; people are influenced by people. It stands a good chance that some of the products you have purchased in the past, you have only bought because someone you know had one and told you how great it was.

Subservient thought pattern

Once isolated from any independent thoughts or external influences, your only source of influence is coming from the sales video itself, keeping you in a subservient mode of acceptance and coercing you to follow prompts to satisfy your new-found desire of obtaining your much wanted product.

Kept from long term thought & ramifications

Of course, the seller doesn't want you to start thinking about the long term and whether or not you can really afford it or if you could possibly warrant spending this kind of cash on their product etc., so they need you to remain in that short-term thinking mode. This is why they sweeten the pot and have that ticking clock in the corner of the screen. Sometimes they will even have a digital readout saying 27 sold in 4 minutes! Only 88 left, hurry! And as you watch a little longer, the 88 turns to 57. Making you desperately dial the number so you can get yours too.

So now you've learned the basics of keeping someone in short-term thinking mode, but the next section is equally as important. What is being said is just as crucial as the way it's being said. In a way you have to keep your subject in a kind of trance, remaining in that short-term thinking mode as you continue to deliver your coercive script. You need the subject absorbing all you are saying and not allowing their mind to wander elsewhere. So as you can imagine, once you've started down this path, your speech patterns should never dramatically change. People are extremely attuned to sensing change in another's behavior. If you suddenly begin to get excited in your speech patterns, or your speed and pitch rise slightly, the subject you are questioning may sense this and begin to wonder why. Then their thoughts are focused on you and what could possibly happen, instead of their thoughts going where you intend on steering them. Let's explore this further.

Below is an account of an event that happened to a friend of mine, James Pyle. James (Jim) is a former army interrogator, and I turned to him for one of his great examples of easing a person into a confession. After reading the details of the event below, which has many great subtle methods of how the confession came about, we will explore some of the science behind the story.

26 April 2022Date

"WELL - UHH, I DON'T KNOW…"

1.ATMOSPHERICS

2012 Pittsburgh, PA, the parents of Mike have just introduced him to my wife and me, stating he is home on leave from the Army. At this time, I am eight years retired from a 20-year career as a Human Intelligence collector, and my wife is still an active-duty Signals Intelligence Army Warrant Officer (WO4). I initiated a conversation with Mike, and it rolled into a most serious situation.

2.CONVERSATION

"Mike, where are you stationed?" I asked. His reply lacked enthusiasm, "Ft Hood Texas." What do you do at Ft Hood?" "I am a small wheel mechanic." "Thank you for your service, and I am sure your parents are glad to have you home for a while." "Yes sir" "When do you have to go back?" "Well – uhh, I don't know…" His eyes dart down, and he turns away and leaves the room. That was a most telling moment in that, without exception, every soldier in the US Army knows exactly when their leave ends as they make the very best of it down to the last minute, and that was the first time I had heard that response to the question, "when do you have to report back to duty?" My wife and I both look at each other, and we know without a doubt that Mike is AWOL (Absent without Leave). We talk with his parents and query how long he has been home, and they indicated about three months. His family had no previous military experience and were not aware that leave much beyond 30 days, especially for young soldiers, is quite rare.

We requested a chance to talk with Mike, and they called him back in, my wife and I having conferred quietly prior to his coming back in, she giving me the lead in this next very serious discussion. "Mike, it appears to me that you have been home for quite some time, and that not knowing when you are due back on duty is out of character for a soldier... you know if you are AWOL, there is a warrant issued that if you are even cited for a traffic violation you can be arrested (holding my hands out together as if cuffed) and sent back to Ft Hood to face a Court Martial!" His parents were shocked; Mike sat eyes cast down and certainly embarrassed at being exposed. I let the room go silent for just a moment and I turned to Mike and said, "Debbie, my wife, and I can help." His head comes up, his parents lean in, and I say: "You're in a serious but manageable situation, Debbie as an Army Officer could take you into custody as we speak, but that won't be necessary if I make a simple phone call to your Company Commander, inform him of your whereabouts and that you are willing to return and do the right thing to fix this problem." I told his parents that the Army would provide transportation back to Ft Hood, TX, he would be held in supervised custody, he would no doubt lose some rank, and most likely chapter him out of military service. Given that he had left without leave, it occurred to me that would be an agreeable option. Given that he and his parents agreed to my proposal, Mike was taken to the bus station, returned to Ft Hood, Tx, held in custody, busted to E-1 in rank, and released from his military service. Mike returned to Pittsburgh, PA. Later we learned that he was actually employed by the US Coast Guard, and all because he did the right thing to fix the wrong thing he had done by being AWOL.

In the above example, Jim did so many things to help the young man in a situation that could have gone completely the other way. If it were not for Jim's vast experience, the whole thing could have gone horribly wrong. For now, though, let's explore some of the things Jim did right (and probably much better than I ever could).

At first, it was Jim's experience that helped him spot there was a problem; it could have been missed by many or looked over, especially by civilians. Jim did not get confrontational or call him out which would have only exacerbated the situation. At this point it would have been easy for friction to build, tensions to mount, and a physical struggle to erupt if they had tried to force the young man into custody. Already having a reasonable level of rapport would have certainly helped, this then allowed Jim to take things a step further.

Making sure not to create a 'me versus you' scenario, Jim went on to put the young man at ease, letting him know that he wasn't alone in this, and gave the appearance that he had options. He made the whole situation seem a lot less harsh, and that handing himself in was the most favorable option (which it probably was). Fear of the unknown can be overwhelming for some, and the fear of not knowing what's going to happen to you if you hand yourself in can be terrifying. Jim helped the young man to feel less isolated and assured him that he could help; he eased the burden and made him feel comfortable with what he was doing. Most importantly, he used a term I love: "This is a fixable problem". Many times people feel they have no other option, and that their situation is dire and beyond repair. Helping them to realize that there is a way out for them is critical. They need to know that this isn't the end.

Having talked to Jim about the situation above, I know there were a lot of other factors in play too. For the moment, however, we have addressed some of the main ones. We will go on to explore more areas that are relevant to extracting a confession to give you more tools in your toolbox and delve deeper into the mechanics of how it works in this section.

Some of the steps to extracting your confession will be as follows, but where the path could split, we will take the first path then go back and revisit the area to see what should be done in the instance of taking the second path. By the end, all of the pieces should come into play for you (like a jigsaw slotting together) and you will have all the necessary knowledge of how to extract a confession.

Step 1. Rapport-building

You need to gain rapport with the subject. By this I don't mean something like, "Hey, nice watch, did you kill Janice?" That's simply not going to work. Finding common ground is great, but for a confession, you need to go a little deeper. First of all, you need to put yourself in their head, looking at things form their point of view. You need to try and imagine what they're going through and empathize as much as is humanly possible. I don't mean you have to forgive; I don't mean you have to condone what they've done, or even agree with what they've done, but you do have to remember that they are human. They're probably scared of what's going to happen, they may feel isolated and alone, like they have nowhere to go, and no will understand them. It's your job to put them at ease. It's down to you to reassure them (we will go into how shortly), and it's down to you to let them know that there is a way out for them. All while making that way out appear less grim than they have probably imagined.

Upon building this rapport and empathizing as much as you can with the subject, you can now move on to step two.

Step 2. Maintaining the relationship.

You have now created the relationship; you must also maintain it. You need to work as hard as possible to let them know that you're there to help them. The last thing you want is to create a "me versus you" scenario. You don't want to be working against them, you want to let them see that you're working with them to try and create the best outcome all round for everyone.

Step 3. Vindicating the act.

Whatever the offense may have been, in the person's mind at the time of committing the act they would have rationalized it. It is your place to now vocalize this justification. This will have the subject in agreeance with you and in the "exactly" frame of mind. This will allow them to save face and will be exceptionally effective in getting them onside, as well as keeping them in the short-term thinking mode. You can use phrases like:

"It's easily done. I've seen people do this kind of thing loads of times. Good people get into situations like this all the time. Your friends help you out, and naturally you want to return the favor. So sometimes you do things you wouldn't normally do. It's understandable. You can easily start off down a path without thinking about where it might lead."

Notice the use of the words "**good** people get into situations" and not "people get into situations; it doesn't make you a **bad** person." This is very deliberate. It is important to keep things positive. Refrain from using negative words. More on this later.

Step 4. Lessening responsibility.

It's easy to blame somebody or something else for an event that was your own fault, especially in the age we live in, where a culture of, "if something bad happens find someone to sue" prevails. With every passing year it seems responsibility on the individual is lowered. Children grow up blaming parents for their life turning out the way it has. If not parents then the school, the government, teachers, society; anything and anyone but themselves. So it becomes increasingly harder to get a person to own up to something. The method here is to utilize this culture of blame game. Spread the fault around a little. Make the subject believe it's not entirely their fault. Blame the world, society, the system, anything you like, and of course the bigger the better. Blaming a small group or an individual might indicate that the subject has the potential to be let off. So you need to keep to the fact that even though it might not be entirely their fault, the action was by them and they have to accept their part in it. As long as you can alleviate the feeling of full responsibility from them, then you're going the right way.

Step 5. Denial prevention.

You may come across denials or some attempt to stop you from moving forward with your work. It is highly important that you put a stop to this. Cut them off mid-sentence. I cannot stress this enough: **you must not let them complete a denial!** It will only serve to make things harder if they get to finish what they are saying, because then you won't be able to offer them the olive branch to save face later on when it comes to the confession part. (Again, I'll show you how to deal with attempts of denial later).

Step 6. Lessening severity.

At this point you want to be moving forward with the mindset that they did it. I'll show you what to do with evidence later too, but that should be saved and only used if it's needed. You want to talk to the subject in a low and steady tone that makes them feel at ease and use carefully chosen words that sound less harsh when talking about the crime. Lessening the severity of the crime will assist you when it comes to the full confession. Instead of using words like "stole" you can say "removed"; instead of saying, "Why did you assault him?" you can say, "How come it ended up becoming a physical disagreement with him?" making the crime sound less heinous. Of course, that doesn't mean it is, it just means you're able to make the subject feel more at ease talking about it.

Step 7. Relieving Isolation.

It's also important that at no point the subject feels isolated. If they feel they have nowhere to turn it can make matters worse. They need to be informed that others have gone through similar situations, and that you've seen and heard it all before. It's nothing new, and you can deal with whatever they have done. Again using phrases like:

"You're not the first to do this kind of thing you know. Loads of people have been in the same situation." or, "There's not a single problem in the world that cannot be fixed or worked out one way or another." and, "I fully understand, and I can assure you that it can be sorted. Plenty of other people have been in the same situation before and it's always been sorted."

This will neatly segue into step 8.

Step 8. Highlighting the Truth.

This is the point where it all comes together. After you've spent the time working to achieve the steps above, you now have to make the subject believe there is nowhere else to go and no other alternative than to tell you the truth. At this point, you want them focused solely on telling you the truth and not on the actual event itself. You need to appear to be offering an olive branch in a situation that would be otherwise helpless. It's crucial that the subject believes the only way out of the predicament is to tell you everything.

You can emphasize this by using phrases like:

"As I said, it's a fixable issue, but the only way I can do anything about it for you, is if we get everything out in the open, so I know what I'm dealing with." or, "The only way I can sort this out is if you tell me everything, so I know exactly what to do next." We're almost full circle, maintaining that rapport and relationship you've built, you now move on to adding to the words used in step four. Like I mentioned from the earlier example, my favorite phrase is now coming into play. You can say things like "It's a fixable problem." Or "It's not the end of the world, we can still put this right." There are so many possible ways to help the subject to see a different viewpoint here, which is what you might need to do. A lot of the time the subject can only see the imminent trouble they're in. They think of the possible punishment that follows, and that's as far as their mind will allow them to go. It's like a great dark stone wall blocks them from seeing the future, and they only see the hypothetical dungeon they're heading towards. It's down to you to let them know that the sun will still rise tomorrow. Life will go on, and they can still "do the right thing".

Step 9. The transition.

Now is the time that you make a smooth transition to the confession. All the time remembering what you have learned earlier on – like the Choice Justification Pyramid and empathizing with the subject, remaining calm, and making them feel at ease. You should have already mentally rehearsed what you'd like to say and have a rough script of where you would like to steer the conversation. Let's take an example of a spy stealing secret government files and use this as a template for our confession.

As you're delivering your script, you might find the person interrupts with an "I did it!" moment and confesses to everything. When this happens, just stop and listen to it all. On the other hand, you may have a subject that requires a little prompting. Now this is once more a vital part of obtaining your confession. You have to be careful yet again with your word choice. Equally as vital as the question is knowing when to ask it. There are giveaway signs that will indicate the optimal time for you, but I'll come to that in a moment. First, let's cover the way in which your question should be structured. Your choice of question style is crucial.

For example, you don't want to ask a question like:

"Did you take and sell the files containing classified information?"

Instead ask something like:

"Do you still have the files?" Or "Where are the files now?"

Replace words like:

"Cheated" with "followed your instincts" Or "had intercourse with."

"Stolen" should be replaced with "took", "picked up", "kept a hold of" or "obtained."

I'm sure you get the idea. For every serious sounding word there is an alternative that is lesser sounding in severity. The choice of words plays a key role in getting your confession. So don't use negative words or words that imply the gravity of a situation. Keep it light and casual.

The first example implies that you don't know for definite that they did it. This might spark the idea in the subject's mind that they can still convince you of their innocence. They might then take it upon themselves to attempt to wriggle out of it and continue to lie or try to convince you they didn't do it.

The second example implies that you know in no uncertain terms what they did, and their only choice is to tell you everything, especially if you've followed the earlier steps correctly.

Now that you have an idea of how to ask the question, let's cover the when. As you're in the process of delivering your script you need to observe closely. Look for signals of compliance and agreement. These might be verbal or non-verbal. They might be as simple as nodding as you talk, or they might agree with particular parts of your script. This is when all of your earlier lessons in body language will pay off. If you've practiced enough, you will be able to spot these tells easily and without giving it away that you've seen their cues. There may also be verbal cues that tell you when the person is ready to confess.

For example, they might say: "That's right, it's not my fault." Or "Yes, I was just trying to do the right thing, and before I knew it I was in over my head."

This is the point where you've hit payday. Now is the time to strike. Don't delay; ask the question, but remember, as always, you must not change your tone, volume, or demeanor. The excitement of getting the confession might have your adrenalin surging, so take a moment, breathe, and calm yourself. Then fire away with the question and prompt the subject to spill the beans.

At the stage of the subject making a confession, it's again extremely crucial that you don't react with any form of retort.

If you suddenly jump up and start yelling, "I knew it! I knew you stole the files!" the subject will feel penalized by you and will more than likely go into a defensive mode again. They will feel betrayed and will no longer be cooperative. You must instead reward the confession to encourage further cooperation. There's no need to go to extremes or treat them with a chocolate biscuit for doing good. A simple "thank you" is sufficient. It's important that the subject feels good about sharing the truth with you and they certainly won't if you're bouncing around the room doing a victory dance like it's your birthday.

As with the previous areas, refrain from changing your tone, volume, or demeanor. Just thank the subject and continue to actively listen to what they have to say as sincerely as you possibly can. It's worth noting here that you should never try to interrogate a person when they are under the influence of drugs or alcohol. As a huge part of your deception spotting relies on reactions, body language, and other factors vital to timing and visual display, all of these factors can be impeded by the use of drugs or alcohol. A person's reaction times might be different; they could become easily confused if they're not thinking clearly. They might display signs they wouldn't normally display down to a lack of physical control, as well as many other factors that could play a part in inhibiting your ability to read that person correctly.

As with any skill, the more you practice, the better you will become, and just like any other skill, it is subject to 'Skill Fade': If you don't continually use it, or put what you've learned into practice, you won't be as proficient as someone who uses it daily. So try to practice what you've learned at least a couple of times a week. Maybe find a complete stranger in a coffee shop and engage in a few minutes of observation as you converse. Look for verbal and non-verbal signs of a lie, just to keep you in practice. Whenever the opportunity presents itself, jump on the chance to interview somebody, or attempt to get to the truth in situations that arise and give you the chance to practice what you've learned. The more you use it, the better you will become.

Stubborn Liars

In the event of getting yourself into a position with a stubborn subject whom you know is lying but want to get the truth from, there is a method you can use which will *wear down* the subject, for want of a better explanation. You see, from the moment a person starts lying, the cognitive load is seriously increased. From the fabrication of the lie to the thought process of comparing it to past events and experiences from the liar's life, right up to the delivery of the lie, everything has to come across as believable, and this is an enduring task for the brain to do all at once. You, however, can use it to your advantage.

Imagine the person has told their version of events, now you can start asking questions, deliberately increasing the cognitive load further. For example, you can ask questions like:

"When you went from the bar to the marina, did you take a bus or a cab?"

Now you add this to what you learned earlier about raising the stakes of the question and watch what happens. The subject now has to think carefully about their answer. There are two ways this can go, each of them with their own set of questions and risks. The subject has to ask themselves things like:

"If I say bus, then were there actually any buses running that night? Are there any possible witnesses on the bus? Where did I get on or off the bus, and at what time? Will all of this marry up with what I have told (the police/my wife) in my statement? Do they know something I don't know? Were there any road closures along the bus route I'm unaware of?" and so much more.

On the other hand, if the subject chooses to say cab:

"What taxi company was it? What was the driver like? Did I book or flag the cab? Where was the pick-up point? Can the taxi company be traced? CCTV? Is it possible there could be a driver witness that might say he dropped me somewhere else? Do they know something I don't?" and so much more once again.

All of these thoughts and many more will be going through the mind of the subject, and if you've raised the stakes enough, they will be thinking very carefully and seriously about the answer. This will probably cause them to slow down, have clunky speech, and stutter. The blink rate will increase, and you will get eye flutters. The levels of discomfort will rise dramatically, and all of the 'tells' you've learned earlier on will start to show.

Once they finally pick an answer, you drill down more and continue with your questions. Say they pick taxi: you can then increase the cognitive load even further with questions like:

"Tell me about the driver. Do you remember anything specific about your journey? We have a list of all the taxi companies in the area, is there anything you'd like us to take into account before we contact them all again to confirm what they've already told us?"

Can you see the psychological tactics used behind that last question? The cognitive load on the subject at this point will be through the roof. And you will know, their physical movements will be less. When people are being truthful, they're more prone to being demonstrative as they talk. They'll make gestures and hand movements as they describe what happened. Being under that amount of cognitive stress will have their brain using all its energy to maintain the lie to the best of their ability, thus reducing the physical movements and keeping them very still and inactive.

The more you continue to increase the cognitive load, the more they will struggle to cope. I have known military interrogators tell me that they've had subjects literally fall asleep in the middle of an interrogation! This has happened purely because the cognitive load on their mind has physically exhausted them.

But wouldn't that happen to anyone? Well, the answer to that is no. A person who is telling the truth can simply recall and relay the information of what happened without all of the stress involved in telling a lie. If someone asks you what you had for breakfast yesterday you can usually answer them without much thought and in a timely fashion, whereas a person who needs to lie about it needs to put a lot of thought into their answer.

"Do I say fried breakfast? Did the cooker stop working and I don't know about it? If I say cereal, did the milk run out 3 days ago and I haven't noticed?"

You see the amount of thought that has to go into telling a simple lie. It's stressful, it's tiring, and it takes a lot of thought. That's why the body will tell you what the words do not.

I hope you can see now how advantageous the body language section is and how relevant it was that you learned it in order to use it with the rest of the methods within this book.

Erratic behavior

Sometimes you might not stop the subject with your system, and when plan number one doesn't work, devise a new little plan and try again. They could freak out and lose their temper, break down and cry, or try any number of other emotional outbursts to attempt to throw you off and prevent you from continuing. So how do you deal with this? Pretty much the same as before. Recognize it, address it, and continue. Make it completely obvious that their little tantrum is not going to work and carry on. So you could say something like:

"I realize you're upset, and believe me, that's the last thing I would ever want. All I want to do is make this easier for you, not harder, but you have to understand that crying isn't going to resolve or change anything. It's not going to get either of us anywhere. So let's get this done and dusted so we can put it behind us and move on." And again, you continue with your script.

Crying is probably one of the easier elements to deal with; when a person gets angry or begins to lose their temper it can be a little more difficult to handle, but they can be managed as long as you remain composed. Don't alter your tone, volume, or demeanor. Stay as you are and, using the same system, gently do the same as before. Recognize it, address it, and move on. You could say something like:

"I understand this must be frustrating for you but getting mad isn't going to help resolve this. The only way to fix this situation is to calmly go through the facts so I can find out your side of the story and get everything sorted out." It is exceptionally important that you do not under any circumstances raise your voice, change your tone, or alter your demeanor at this point. You must remain calm and level-headed. You have to be cool, keep control of the situation, and as before, when you've addressed the outburst, carry on with your script.

The majority of the time, any display of erratic behavior will result in a confession not long after. It seems that the emotional outburst is a kind of last resort, and when the subject realizes that it didn't work, the reality sets in that they have no other cards left to play. As soon as the realization of the fact that they have no other option sinks in, the confession quickly follows.

Backtracking slightly, I'd like to cover how to deal with objections and denials. As you go through your script, you may find that a subject might attempt to deny any activity in what you're saying or interrupt with a denial. They'll generally try to cut in with: "I already said..." Or "I told you before..." The key here is to cut it short and prevent it from going any further straight away.

A rapid response is important. You can usually stop a person dead in their tracks using only one word: their name. It's a natural reaction to stop talking when someone calls your name; it's natural to listen to them and see what they want. Have you ever been walking around a busy city and stopped in your tracks to turn around and look because you thought you heard someone call your name? It's a very effective method to take control of the conversation. You state their name firmly but not aggressively. No need to shout, just firmly state their name and continue to validate the person so you don't break the rapport and avoid creating that "you versus me" scenario we mentioned. As soon as you say their name you continue with:

"I know what you're about to say is very important to you, and I promise we will cover anything you have to discuss. We will come back to it, but right now I just want to establish a few facts..." or whatever the next part of your script is. Then, just continue with your script unfazed, as if it had never happened. Hopefully, you have followed the earlier steps and have the subject in a nice, calm atmosphere where they don't feel the need to start yelling. You simply keep them in this frame of mind as you progress, constantly observing for body language and other cues that you have learned which indicate that the person is at ease and not becoming agitated.

Once again, I need to stress that at no point should you attempt to raise the volume of your voice here. This will only cause friction in the situation. The subject will then begin viewing you as an opponent instead of being there to help them and offer a way out. You need the subject to truly believe you are on their side and their only option is to divulge the truth to you.

A second way to regain control of the conversation, and silence the subject's attempt of denial, is to simply put your hand up in front of you like your stopping traffic. It needs to be done in a very abrupt but non-offensive way. You don't want to display aggression or any kind of attitude when you do this. More of a friendly crossing patrol officer's indication to stop and wait. Many people are surprised at how effective raising your hand can be to halt a person's speech pretty much immediately. Again, as soon as you're in control of the conversation, you can address the attempt at interruption and carry on with your script.

With the above listed methods of preventing you from continuing addressed and extinguished, you can carry on with your script as long as you need to. There is no set time limit. Each time you do it, the time it takes will vary. The only thing you need to know is that no matter what, you simply continue. If the other person remains silent, that's a good thing. The more they hear your script repeated over and over with the use of slightly different terminology each time, the more likely the acceptance will be, and the more likely you will achieve your goal. As I mentioned before in the part about sales videos, the more we see or hear something, the more likely we are to accept it. This is why affirmations work so well. So persist with your script as many times as required until the subject either volunteers a confession or you feel the time is right to ask a test question.

Most important is knowing when to shut up: when the subject is finally telling you everything, keep your mouth shut! You may at times prompt them to continue, or help to make them feel at ease, but let them keep talking. You can even ask questions about particular events as you go, but don't take over the speech! Any questions should be quick, any prompts should be short; just softly saying things like "go on" with a nod, reassuring them that what they're doing is good and to continue.

So in summary, you must:

1) Gain rapport

2) Let them know you want to help

3) Vindicate the act

4) Lessen responsibility

5) Stop any denials

6) Continue on the premise that they did it

7) Relieve feelings of isolation

8) Highlight the truth

9) Transition to a confession

Repeat steps 6, 7, 8, & 9 as needed (only if required).

You may need to adjust the delivery slightly depending upon the situation, but the method should pretty much stay the same each time. Whether it's a hardened criminal or a cheating spouse, the theory holds. Adjust the wording accordingly and plan on delivering each step to work towards the truth. In the next section, you learn the all-important question to ask when they've finished spilling the beans.

18. The Most Important Question to Ask at the End of a Confession

The most important question to ask at the end of a confession is: Did I press record?! Just kidding, it's actually, "Why should I believe you?" When you have asked this, remain silent, because the answer is critical. You are listening out for something very specific here, and if the answer is anything but what you're about to learn then it stands a very high chance they're lying to you.

What you are listening out for is "because it's the truth." Or some very similar version of those words. Like "because it's true." or "because I'm telling the truth." Anything else should raise red flags immediately. This goes back to the psychology behind liars inherently not wanting to lie. So if they answer with some form of evasive response that would normally pacify the average person, then something's very wrong.

If you get an answer like, "You can ask anyone, they'll all back me up." or they answer with a question like, "why would I lie to you?" or "what do you think?" none of these are acceptable, and none of them answer the question in the way you want it answered. Remember when we looked into distraction, and I gave you methods to remain laser-focused on the goal? This is one of the areas in which you need to apply it. You need to remain fixated on hearing the words "because it's true" and nothing else. Don't allow yourself to be fobbed off with anything other than that reply.

It's also important to add here that after a confession of any sorts you should not have made an enemy, quite the opposite in fact. They should be thanking you for helping them out and offering them a solution or a way out. I'm not suggesting that you should be making best friends for life, but you need to have left them feeling better than you found them.

Upon first contact they might have been feeling like there's no way out, and they have no options, and upon leaving they should feel as though you've opened the door for them to move through to the next chapter of their life. This won't always be the case, but as long as this is where you strive to be, and your aim is to help them through, not to penalize them, then you're doing it right.

If you've delivered the process properly there should be zero resentment and no ill feeling whatsoever. The outcome should feel like the subject has been alleviated of a burden and you helped them to achieve it. Even if you walk away and never see each other again, they should feel gratitude towards you and not animosity.

Of course in a professional capacity, this also helps to reduce the possibility of vengeance attacks in the future from the subject feeling bitter and having the time to stew. If ill feeling is allowed to fester, and the person is holding you responsible, then no good can come of it. You want to be able to sleep at night without concerns that anyone from released or escaped prisoners to ex-partners are on the warpath for you.

It's not all doom and gloom; I've heard of cases where prisoners of war have ended up shaking hands with their interrogator by the end of the session and thanking them for helping them. A lot of the time it's their fears and emotions that need calming, and if you're there to assure them that it's not the end of the world, they will almost certainly feel gratitude towards for you getting them through a very tough time.

19. Busting Myths

Number 1. Men vs Women

Thames House, home of the British Security Service, better known as MI5, has a large crest on the wall with the quote "Regnum Defende" at the bottom. The translation from Latin means 'In Defense of the Realm'. The exterior of the building contrasts with the modern interior. There is glass everywhere, and even the modern office chairs are color-coded to signify a person's position within their department. The offices in the center overlook the atrium, but a window position looking out onto the River Thames is the most sought after. The teams work in conjunction with each other and other agencies extremely effectively, but the staff frequently joke with each other saying "Rectum Defende!" Or in other words, "cover ones ass!" When a trade is built on espionage and lies, it is essential that these traits never spill over into areas where your honesty is paramount. Women are generally more capable of gaining access to prohibited areas and being able to manipulate a situation. That is why they are frequently used as honey traps. The myth that women are better at spotting lies than men though, is just that. Women are better at reading and profiling people, as well as using intuition when it comes to judgement on a person, mostly being more accurate with their abilities to decide if a person is trustworthy or not. When it comes to the actual spotting of specific deception or highlighting a particular lie, the rumor they are better is not necessarily true. There is no supporting evidence for this and in fact, tests have indicated that in this area, men are usually the ones slightly better when it comes to spotting liars. Which can be a little concerning, as there is also evidence to suggest that the people who are the most dishonest and tell the most lies, are also the ones better at spotting liars too!

Number 2. Psychopaths are the Best Liars

This is again untrue; however, they can frequently be highly intelligent, giving them the edge when it comes to being able to control or manipulate a situation or person. As for the ones that are not as highly educated, they still tend to be charming, steering us towards wanting to believe them. This section may seem like I'm stereotyping which, admittedly, I am a little. Even though I am moderately generalizing, the majority of (although not all) psychopaths do fit into this category. I'm hoping now that I won't end up creating a huge debate and also start a contest regarding the difference between a psychopath and a sociopath. I'll let you work that one out for yourself.

As a matter of interest, extroverts find it easier to lie than introverts. They lie more frequently and feel more comfortable about lying in comparison to the largely uncomfortable feeling introverts experience when telling a lie.

Number 3. There are truth serums that can make you tell anyone everything

The famous chemical Sodium Pentothal, more commonly known as a truth serum, is another myth made famous by spy movies and detective novels. It's not entirely without some form of truth behind it, though, no pun intended. The original concept was formed by Dr Robert House. In around 1915 he administered a drug called Scopolamine to pregnant women during childbirth. He noticed that, as well as eliminating pain and inducing drowsiness, it had another strange effect on his patients too. It would cause them to speak automatically without thinking, they would also respond without thought to any questions they were asked. His thoughts went to the idea of prisoners who when interrogated continued to claim their innocence. Other versions of the drug have been tried and tested but Scopolamine has the added benefit of not only wiping the memory of the session with the subject but also the few moments before the session begun. Various government agencies have trialed it as well as tested it on captured spies and, in some instances, even their own agents! But does it work? Well, kind of. You see it makes a subject extremely obliging. They become dazed and compliant and simply say whatever they think the person questioning them wants to hear. A bit like being drunk. Sometimes, when a person is drunk, they say all types of things which may or may not be true. Eventually, the Supreme Court ruled that confessions obtained under the influence of any kind of truth serum were coerced, making the use of truth serums unconstitutional. Therefore, the bottom line is that overall, they don't really work. You may get told what you want amongst a mass of other information, but there is no way of saying for sure if it's definitely true, or if the subject is simply telling you what you want to hear. On top of that, if a person is in a position where they have real reasons for withholding certain information no matter what, then there is a high chance that they won't reveal it anyway. So the silver bullet theory of a chemically induced confession which can be obtained from anyone is indeed a fallacy.

Number 4. People Fold their Arms When they're Lying

This seems to be one of the most common statements I so frequently come across. It is true that the folding of the arms in some instances can be considered a defensive stance. It is also true that some people fold their arms when they feel threatened or uncomfortable. At the same time, it's true that some people simply fold their arms because they feel comfortable and relaxed that way. I know this because I'm one of them. As I have mentioned before, there is no singular physical act that a person can do to definitively indicate a lie. It is only when you have established a baseline that you can observe a person and consider whether or not that particular action is not one of their usual habits. Even then, it doesn't necessarily indicate they are lying. It can simply mean they are uncomfortable with the topic or situation etc. Your lessons on congruency should kick in here and give you a better perspective on what the person might be thinking or feeling.

Number 5. People get angry when they lie - The Freeze

People can definitely get angry when lying, but not always. It's not a definitive way of spotting deception. Sometimes a person can be getting angry with just cause. On the flipside though, there is something that can be louder than a person shouting, "silence!"

I have said multiple times to several people, "Silence can sometimes be the loudest shout of guilt." This particular method is useful for spotting deceit, especially when several people might possibly be guilty. Have you ever seen any of the Poirot movies by Agatha Christie? Usually, at the end of the movie he gathers everyone into a room and goes about divulging the ways in which he deduced who was the killer. A few red herrings are eliminated and eventually, the least suspected person who has remained silent the whole time is the one that is proved to be the murderer. Other characters might protest or question Hercule Poirot, but it's usually the one who remains silent who turns out to be the guilty party.

Now as dramatic as all this may seem, I can give you an example of how you can adapt this to fit everyday life when I explain the method itself to you entirely. Imagine five students living in a house. One is about to get into the shower and the other four are downstairs watching The Big Bang Theory in the living room. As student number one is about to get under the running water, he grabs his shampoo, and the bottle is empty. He knows there was at least half left when he used it last, so he wraps a towel around himself and runs downstairs into the living room. As he bursts in, he shouts:

"Who's used all of my shampoo?"

Students 1, 2 and 3 all shrug and say things like: "Not me" or "I don't know." But student number 4 sits silently. Not only silently but deadly still. This is The Freeze! It's a primitive way of not attracting attention to yourself. While the rant goes on and his fellow students deny the use of the shampoo, student 4 sits still, frozen to the spot, waiting for the outburst to end and the student whose shampoo is gone to go back upstairs and finish showering.

This Freeze is an indication of guilt. They will often sit silently avoiding eye contact and in some extremes will sometimes begin to do what we call "Turtle Necking." This is where they slowly raise their shoulders a tad and their head sinks slowly down as if it's retracting, like that of a turtle.

So remember, it's not always what's said that indicates a lie, sometimes it's what's not said!

Number 6. People avoid eye contact when lying

We did cover this earlier, but just to reiterate, people don't necessarily break eye contact when lying, in fact most of the time, quite the opposite. I know this may seem counter-intuitive, but the liar will be watching you closely; they want to get as much information as they possibly can in an attempt to read your reaction and see if you believe them or not. It actually indicates a higher chance that they're lying if they're watching you closely as they speak and continue to do so after they've finished speaking.

20. Bonus - Beating a Polygraph Lie Detector Machine

Over the years, there have been several occasions on which I have had to complete a polygraph lie detector test. The ironic thing is, the same organization that required me to undertake these frequent tests were the same people who taught me how to beat them! The instrument for training at the time was a Stoelting UltraScribe - The Arthur VI Polygraph lie detector. It was reasonably old then, so it's probably an antique now! The theory, however, stays the same. After the initial training period, operatives were required to take frequent tests, as well as some not so frequent refreshers, in beating the polygraph. The equipment used for the actual live tests was much more up to date and I think designed and built in-house. Being the kind of person I am, I was intrigued to see if the same methods learned in training on the old machine would still work on a real test with the latest equipment. Luckily for me, it did! Which saved me a lot of paperwork and time in a small room getting 'ahem' "interviewed", shall we say.

Now before we go much further, I need to establish a few facts. Firstly, the very name commonly used for a polygraph machine "The Lie Detector" is itself a lie! There is not a single machine in the world that can definitively detect when a person is lying. A more appropriate name for the machine would be a "Fear Detector". The machine can detect elevations in breathing (as well as stomach breathing vs chest breathing), perspiration, heart rate, pulse, and blood pressure to give an indication of the level of fear related to a particular question or subject. Add this to the perception that the person strapped in is rigged up to what they believe to be a "Lie Detector", and the fear elevates even more, thus giving the examiner more prominent signals of when you might be telling a fib.

The next thing you need to know is that a polygraph machine at best, is still only 60 to 80% accurate. Add to all this the fact that the final reading of the graph itself (to decide whether or not the subject was lying) is ultimately read by a human. So, a machine that isn't even accurate, calibrated by a human with its results still being subject to human judgement and error makes it little more than elaborate guesswork. Now don't get me wrong, I'm not saying that an experienced polygraph expert couldn't work out from the machine if the average person is lying or not, but there's a reason they're not used in courts of law. They are not considered to be accurate enough!

Another point is that some people simply get nervous or anxious in different ways to others. A gentleman I know from Nebraska called Marc is an absolute top-notch worker, but for some reason he crumbles during any interview process. He's excellent at any job he does but just can't cope at the interview stage. For this reason, and the fact that some people are just better at controlling their emotions etc., the polygraph machine cannot ever be 100% accurate.

So how does man beat machine? Well, there are actually several ways, but I'll let you know what the easiest are.

So down to business, how is it done? Well in order to understand how to beat the machine, you have to understand how the machine works first. The theory is reasonably simple; the machine measures your vital signs, like pulse rate etc., and these signs "spike" when you tell a lie. Now at the beginning of the test the examiner will ask sample questions that he will expect you to lie to. These are sometimes called "Control Questions". For example, "Have you ever stolen anything?" or "have you ever cheated at a game?" These questions will set the base line for indicators of a lie later on in the test. Now because you know these are test questions, and because you know the examiner knows you're lying and you both know at this point, it's fine to do so; your vitals won't spike as high as they are likely to if you lie later on in the test.

Identify the types of questions you're asked

There are three basic types of questions you will be asked: relevant, irrelevant, and control.

Irrelevant questions are those that are obvious, such as, "What is your name?" or "Am I wearing a suit?" Relevant questions are the important ones, such as, "Did you sell classified information," or "Have you ever given access to secret material to anybody not authorized to do so?" Control questions are those to which your reactions will be compared against the relevant questions. These are usually questions that pretty much everybody can answer "yes" to, but which most people will feel uncomfortable answering honestly. For example: "Have you ever told a lie?" or "Have you ever been untruthful to your employer about your reason for being late/absent?" When you know the difference between these questions you have an advantage and can react accordingly.

At the start of the test when the examiner asks the sample questions, simply make your vitals spike by biting your tongue as you are about to answer the question. This will cause the machine to register your initial spikes as quite high. Now, in order for anything else to be considered a lie, the machine will have to measure your vitals as going above the spikes it set at the beginning with the sample questions. Of course, it won't, because you won't be biting your tongue when you answer any of the other questions, and now whatever you respond with, the machine will consider to be true!

You can also think of something extremely mentally stressful, or if you have a phobia, like a fear of spiders for example, you can imagine spiders crawling all over you during the process of answering the test questions. This again will cause your vitals to spike if done correctly.

As with most of the training I've received, one method is never enough, and I have generally been taught two or more methods for every possible situation. As usual I will extend that courtesy and do the same for you. So here goes with the second method.

Now this second method does take a little practice, however, it can be more effective with the newer technology that measures changes in other areas, like your eyes! (Pupil Dilation Measurements.) Whereas you might be able to change your pulse rate and make your vitals spike on demand, your eyes are not so easily controlled.

So here goes with method two: You have to put yourself into a trance state. Now I'm not talking like an undead zombie mode where you dribble and groan or anything crazy like that; it's much more simple. I can pretty much guarantee you've done it before. Have you ever been reading, watching TV, or concentrating on something, when a person in the same room asks you if you want a cup of coffee, or would you like a pizza for dinner, and you've answered yes or no on autopilot? Well, that's the kind of trance state I'm talking about. All you need to do to achieve it is to replay a favorite movie in your head, or concentrate on something you know intimately enough to occupy your mind, while still being aware of what is happening in the room and answering on autopilot. You'll always remain aware and always answer the way you should but without alerting the machine as to whether your answers are truthful.

Now as I said, this way does take a little practice, as you can be brought out of a trance state as quickly (if not quicker) than you can go into one. If the examiner were to bang his hand on the table, or someone suddenly were to enter the room, for example. However, these same actions will also cause your signs to spike. So, in order to return accurate results, the examiner would need to allow for your heart rate etc. to settle again, giving you the required time to get back into your trance state. All you have to do is practice bringing the trance state on as quickly as possible. Have a favored method or a default thought system you can refer to straight away. That way you won't have to waste the first 60 seconds trying to think of a film you know well enough to replay in your head all the way through.

Another little point worth making is not to forget that the examiners themselves are trained to look for deception. On top of this, examiners are known to use mind games and tricks to assist in the whole process. The machine measures perspiration via the fingertips, so examiners have been known to ask you to wash your hands or hand you a wet wipe, asking if you'd mind wiping your fingertips. The idea is that they convince you, that in order to get the accurate reading they need, they must make sure all traces of perspiration are removed from the beginning. Then they might check to see if you have actually washed your hands, or closely observe as you use the wet wipe to see if you miss any particular areas. If they check the bathroom after you're supposed to have used it to wash your hands and find the basin is bone dry, the soap unused and no paper towels in the waste basket, this will give an indication that you don't want the machine to be as accurate as it can be and possibly have something to hide.

There is usually a pre-test interview and a post-test interview to contend with as well. During the pre-test interview the examiner might try to convince you of the accuracy of the machine or use a selection of psychological tactics to instill fear into you. For example, they might say that new information has come to light just before the interview, and you'll find out what it is during the test.

The post-test interview will be to look for differences in your behavior and composure. They will be watching carefully and making mental notes of your physiology. The examiner might also leave the room for quite some time and come back, giving the impression they have caught you out in a lie. They might try and bluff you with a question like: "In the process of the test I asked you if you'd ever seen documentation you were not authorized to see, and you answered no. Would you like to change your answer before the final report is submitted?" This trick has caught many people out and is simply a bluff; don't fall for it and stick to your guns. If they knew for definite you were lying, they wouldn't be asking you the question.

During the interview the polygrapher's eyes will constantly be moving between the machine and you. The reason for this is simple; it's they who have to make the final call, not the machine. So instead of thinking about how is man going to beat machine? Change your thinking to "how do I beat the examiner?" It's he or she who will be watching you and have the final say on whether they believe you or not. Therefore, it's them you have to convince that you're telling the truth. Like I said, before, during, and after the official interview, they will be watching your every move and studying you carefully, so give them reason to believe you're an honest and truthful person all the way through the process, before it starts and after it ends. Because although the machine might get unhooked, and you might have finished, the examiner certainly hasn't.

Finally, if you want a little extra assurance that you'll walk away from the test without any problems, you can always mix the two methods by biting your tongue for the sample questions and then putting yourself into a trance state as well to ensure your vitals don't spike during the test.

For reference, the best way to avoid failing a polygraph test is not to take one. In the private sector in the US, you cannot be fired for refusing to take a polygraph test. This does not apply to Government employees, however.

21. Conclusion

I hope by now you've got to grips with how each of the disciplines we've covered in this book add up to what I call Combined Communication Analysis (C.C.A.). This is when all the Statement Analysis, psychology, body language, and other factors like tone, pitch, blink rate, physical and verbal tells, eye movement, stress signals, establishing a baseline, and most importantly, incongruence and clusters of any combination of the above are taken in to account. In short, deception detection is in the business of change. You're looking for what has changed from the norm. Anything that isn't normally there needs to be noted, and clusters of these "tells" are a high indication that something's not as it should be and needs looking into further.

Years of practice has me at an advantage over most, however, I can still make mistakes (I'm only human, contrary to popular belief), so don't expect to get to this page and be an instant expert. Start where I told you to; learn it one step at a time, and most importantly, practice. Practice all the time and keep practicing as much as you can. As I mentioned earlier, I don't like to use still images because people don't stand around in a pose waiting for you to read their body language. Movements and actions are fluid, fleeting, and sometimes gone in a glance. This is where you need to go out into the world and watch people, have bets with yourself, and if you feel awkward watching people, start with videos. There's plenty to choose from online and of course, politicians are always a good place to start. They lie a lot, and their body language shows it.

Other forms of practice can include watching the people around you at work or observing people in the line when you're waiting to pay for your shopping. Look for the obvious signs that they're getting impatient when the lady with the purse full of coupons finally gets to the point of paying and is still looking for her credit card. Make a mental note of what you see, then look for the same signs in your daily life and see if they correspond with what you've seen at the shopping store. Look for trade professionals like mechanics giving a quote and watch the way they tell their customer what they think the problem is and how much it will cost. Can you tell if they're being open and honest, or are they pushing their luck for a slightly bigger payment? Watch people in their natural environments and decide if any of their actions look out of the ordinary and if so, why? Making this an habitual part of your everyday life will continually increase your ability to be able to read people. With practice you'd be surprised at how rapidly you can become extremely attuned to the people around you and gain the ability to accurately read them. I highly suggest watching a video on YouTube where Orson Wells talks about his experience in Cold Reading while stuck at an airport for the day to demonstrate exactly how good you can become and how quickly you can achieve it. And finally, if you would like to take things further, then please visit my website to get more information and details about training.

Thank you for reading and best of luck in the future with your new skills to know HOW TO TELL IF SOMEONE IS LYING.

If you enjoyed this book, please consider leaving a review. It really helps authors and can also influence others when it comes to a decision to make the purchase. It is highly appreciated, and I thank you in advance.

Printed in Great Britain
by Amazon